Johnny Harris
Restaurant
Cookbook

Johnny Harris
Restaurant
Cookbook

JULIE DONALDSON
LOWENTHAL

photography by

MARY BRITTON SENSENEY

PELICAN PUBLISHING COMPANY
Gretna 2014

ISBN: 9781455618965
E-book ISBN: 9781455618972

Produced by Pinafore Press / Janice Shay
Food styling by Marian Cooper Cairns
Index by Sara LeVere

Additional photography:
Katie McGee, p. 25
Julie Lowenthal, pp. 130, 206
Courtesy of the Georgia Historical Society,
pp. 13, 15, 20, 31

Printed in China

Published by Pelican Publishing Company, Inc.
1000 Burmaster Street, Gretna, Louisiana 70053

This book is dedicated to my loving parents,
Yvonne and Phil Donaldson.

To Mom, for your constant love, support, being the
most stylish mom I know, and for being my best friend.

To Dad, for without your tireless
pursuit of fresh new ideas and continued
passion and vision for success in business—as well
as in life—this would not be possible.

"*famous for fine foods*"

JOHNNY
HARRIS
AIR CONDITIONED

JUST THE PLACE
FOR YOUR PARTY
PHONE 8290
FOR RESERVATIONS

JOHNNY HARR

East Victory Drive
Savannah, Georgia

Established 1924

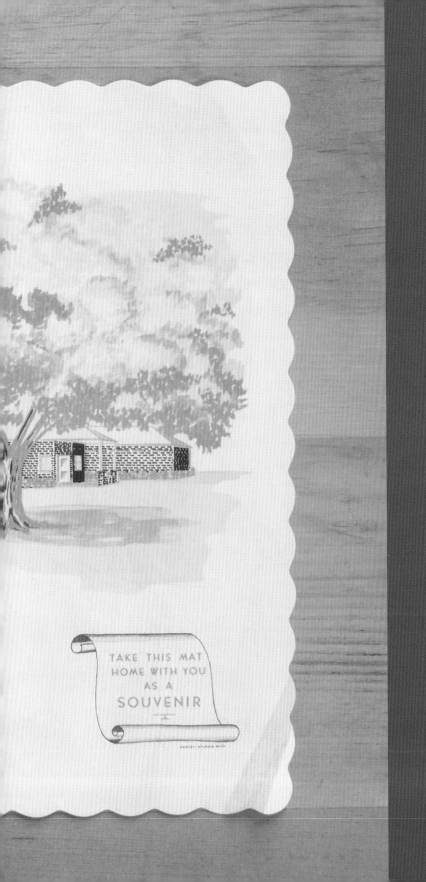

TAKE THIS MAT
HOME WITH YOU
AS A
SOUVENIR

OUR HISTORY

John Newman Harris was born on November 30, 1889, in Petersburg, Virginia, in Dinwiddie County, about 25 miles south of Richmond. His father was a jeweler. John had two brothers, William and Richard, and a sister, Mary. He graduated from high school in Petersburg in 1908 and attended one year of college before he moved to Savannah, Georgia. When he was settled he told his sister, Mary Harris, "I have been seduced, and I have fallen in love with a beautiful lady named Savannah, and want you to know that I plan to spend the rest of my life with her." Johnny Harris knew even then that he had found his home. His charisma and determination to become successful led him to be a good student and a hard worker. By 1917, at the age of 29, he had established a profitable grocery and poultry farm in Savannah. However, he already had his sights set on his next venture.

In the spring of 1924, Harris built a little roadside diner and named it Johnny Harris Tavern and Bar-B-Cue Restaurant. It was located on the corner of Bee Road and Victory Drive (formerly named Estill Avenue), which was about halfway between the main city and the small village of Thunderbolt, home to many commercial and private fishing boats.

In the early 1900s, Estill Drive was a dirt road and considered a suburban area of Savannah, being well away from Savannah's historic downtown. In 1908, the United States of America became the first country outside of France to host an automobile race using the name Grand Prix (or "Grand Prize"). The race was run in Savannah along Estill Avenue. In 1919, Estill Avenue was renamed Victory Drive and was planted with beautiful grass medians, lined with palmetto trees. The name change to Victory Drive was a memorial to all the servicemen and women from Chatham

Early photos, clockwise from top: Johnny Harris Tavern and Bar-B-Cue; portrait of Johnny Harris; and the "new" Johnny Harris Restaurant

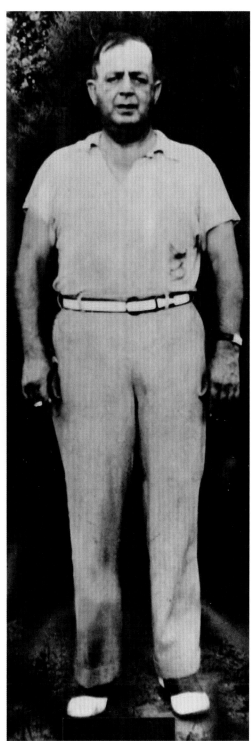

County who were killed during WWI.

This first Johnny Harris Tavern and Bar-B-Cue was a modest, white wooden barbecue "shack," with black shutters, sawdust on the floors, and a tall white wooden fence on one side. Parking for cars was in front and alongside the restaurant. The tavern featured slot machines for entertainment and was a comfortable place for customers to enjoy a meal and have a beer or two. Mr. Harris selected this location

A young Red Donaldson, date unknown.

hoping to attract customers traveling to and from the Savannah Yacht Club at Thunderbolt, the Thunderbolt Casino and Amusement Park (which was destroyed by fire in 1930), and beautiful Bonaventure Cemetery. It was also a handy stop on the way to Tybee Island beach and the resorts of Wilmington Island. It proved to be a wise choice.

In 1925, John Moore, a black cook from Virginia who worked for Johnny Harris, helped Harris create the original Johnny Harris Bar-B-Cue sauce recipe, and it was an immediate hit with the customers who thought it went perfectly with the two specialties on the menu: barbecue pork and fried chicken. The recipe was not written down but was memorized by Moore and Harris, who later put it to paper and shared it with family members and business associates. Customers became so fond of the sauce that they would often bring empty liquor or soda bottles and jars and request to buy extra sauce for their use at home. This same sauce has been made and used in the restaurant for 90 years, and has been bottled and sold since the late 1950s throughout the Southeast and shipped world-wide.

Less than three years after opening the restaurant, Harris was in need of additional

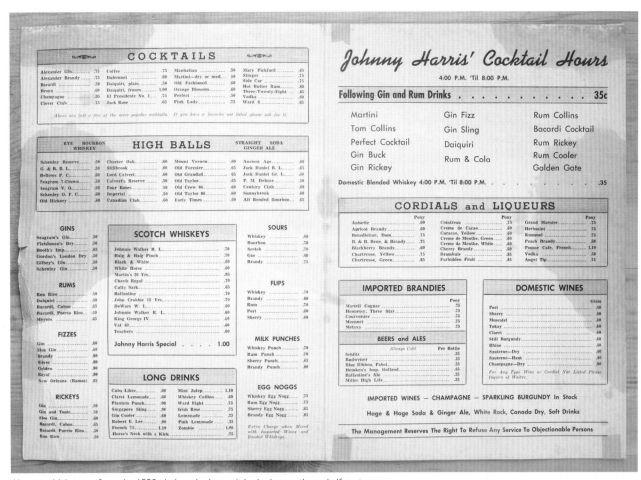

Above, a drink menu from the 1950s; below, the bar as it looked more than a half-century ago.

Nightly music during the '30s, late '40s, and '50s drew large crowds of well-dressed dancers, as in this 1936 photo, to this popular supper club.

help and, in 1927, he hired 18-year-old Kermit Lynnwood Donaldson, who had left his family farm in Bulloch County to find work in Savannah. Donaldson's early duties included dishwashing, cooking, cleaning, tending the barbecue pit, and manning the cash registers. He was a hard worker, walking to the tavern in all kinds of weather and working long days. Harris had a former employee named "Red," and he kept accidentally calling Kermit "Red," until eventually the nickname stuck.

Because these were the "Roaring Twenties," business grew rapidly and Donaldson became indispensable. For his dependability and loyalty, he was rewarded by Harris and given the management of the tavern.

CORKAGE CHARGE
ON
ALL BEVERAGES BROUGHT
INTO THIS BUILDING

•

MINIMUM CHECK CHARGE
/oo 50c PER PERSON

•

GENTLEMEN
NOT PERMITTED TO DANCE
WITHOUT THEIR COATS

Despite the Depression years of the 1930s (or perhaps because of it), Johnny Harris Tavern became so popular and profitable that by 1933, Harris decided to build a much larger, full-service dining establishment and night club. With the end of Prohibition, Harris now had the ability to fulfill his dream of building the finest supper club in Savannah. He purchased six building lots just east of the original location, and in 1935 construction began on a much larger, more modern Johnny Harris Restaurant.

The new restaurant that Red helped build opened for business in the fall of 1936 at its present location at 1651 East Victory Drive. Harris had overseen every aspect of the design and construction. Family and friends said he was "always in full control" when it came to decisions involving his family or the restaurant.

Johnny's plan for the modern red-brick building included three separate dining rooms. The first was the intimate Maple Room Tavern, with a fancy bar; then there

The service buttons still found in each booth can be used to summon a waiter.

was a casual dining section affectionately called The Kitchen, which had booths that allowed customers to view the original slow-cooking barbeque pit; and the crowning glory was a very large, nearly circular Grand Ballroom with a large domed ceiling, 30 feet high. This room was designed for dancing and gaming (the restaurant had many slot machines which were legal until around 1950, when gambling was declared illegal in Georgia) and would fulfill Harris's dream of having the finest supper club in the city.

The circular Grand Ballroom/Dining Room sported 21 spacious handmade cypress wood booths around its perimeter, each with enough room to seat six guests comfortably. The booths featured individual call buttons which were used to summon waiter service. Originally, each booth also had custom-made curtains for additional privacy; however, the curtains were later removed because of complaints that too many amorous incidents were taking place behind them. During Prohibition, customers were allowed to bring in their own liquor but paid a corkage charge for "set-ups."

Postcards celebrated the new palm-lined Victory Drive and Johnny Harris Restaurant and its famous barbecue.

DINING ROOM

JOHNNY HARRIS RESTAURANT

East Victory Drive

SAVANNAH, GEORGIA

BAR-BE-CUE PIT

Red Donaldson and his wife, Maude. Below, Red Donaldson checks one of the vats of Bar-B-Cue sauce at the new factory in early 1950.

During this period, Johnny Harris Restaurant was frequently referred to as a "speakeasy."

The new restaurant could accommodate about 200 customers. Total cost of this new all-brick Savannah showplace in 1936 was less than $50,000, which Harris paid in cash. When the restaurant opened in 1936, the minimum check charge per person was 50 cents. By 1940, the per person charge had increased to one dollar.

In the center of the ballroom was a revolving bandstand that was originally designed with a central column built to look like a revolving lighthouse. That feature eventually became the structure that housed the air conditioning, making the restaurant the first in the Southeast to be air conditioned. Musical groups provided live music while delighted patrons would dance under the "stars"—referring to the hundreds of twinkling lights that were installed in the high domed ceiling, which was painted to resemble a nightime sky.

To further enhance the formal dining room, Harris hired a talented, but unemployed artist—in fact, he had just been released from prison—to paint a colorful mural featuring outdoor scenes around the entire perimeter of the huge Grand Ballroom. This turned out to be a perfect complement to the twinkling stars on the ceiling above. As payment for his work, the artist requested free meals from Johnny Harris during the time it took him to finish the mural. It took more than one year to complete, and received rave reviews from the customers. His name has been forgotten over the years, but his work is still admired.

Many nationally known bands and combos were contracted to play at Johnny Harris Restaurant. This was the big band era, when evening gowns and tuxedos were commonplace on Saturday nights at a supper club. Proper attire was required to dine in the main ballroom, and the restaurant kept a coat closet full of ties and jackets that were available for men who may have not come prepared.

All during the 1930s, '40s and '50s, Harris hired many wellknown big bands to play dance music into the early morning hours. These included Lester Lanin, Warren Covington's Tommy Dorsey Orchestra, Ray Anthony, and Louis Prima, just to name a few. Johnny Harris loved all kinds of music, especially popular music of the day, which was always playing on the restaurant jukebox. During this same period, many of Johnny Harris's younger customers would frequently use the expression, "Let's go jukin' at Johnny Harris on Saturday night!"

One of the first regular live musical performances at Johnny Harris Restaurant was in the 1930s when Johnny hired George Rody, Sr., an accordion player, and his wife Jackie, who had a vaudeville touring act, to perform for his restaurant patrons on a regular basis. The Rodys gave up their road trips, settled in Savannah, and performed for delighted customers at Johnny Harris's for many years. George Rody, Sr., opened an accordion school in Savannah, which eventually became Rody's Music store for aspiring musicians looking for supplies. Other Savannah musicians who played at Johnny Harris's were organist Dana Pelki; Gene Taggart, a wellknown bandleader

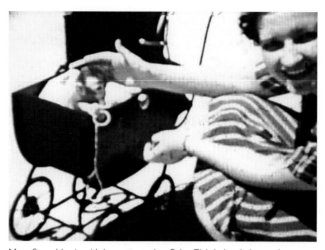
Mary Syms Harris with her pet monkey, Baby Girl, in her baby carriage.

who entertained there for 29 years; Ken Palmer, who has been described as one of the greatest jazz pianists and composers that Savannah has ever seen; the Bob Conn and Robert Taylor Combos; and Buddy Owens on guitar.

In early 1937, Harris created a small zoo behind the restaurant, featuring monkeys, exotic birds, and other animals gathered by Harris on various hunting trips. The back lot soon became a popular attraction with customers and tourists, especially those with children. Johnny Harris and his wife, Mary Syms Harris, loved animals so much that Mary took one of the orphaned baby rhesus monkeys home and raised it as a family pet, naming it "Baby Girl." She would dress it in a bonnet and diapers and push Baby Girl in a baby carriage around the neighborhood, much to the delight of the neighborhood children, who came to refer to Mary as "The Monkey Lady." The Johnny Harris zoo was in operation from 1937 until after Harris's death in 1942.

On April 25, 1942, at age 54, John Newman Harris died of heart disease at Central of Georgia Hospital in Savannah. However, his Johnny Harris Restaurant continued to operate under very strict terms outlined in his will. In it, Kermit Lynnwood "Red" Donaldson was named executor of the estate and general manager of the restaurant. The will also specified that Red Donaldson, Johnny's "good friend and faithful employee," would become a part-owner only if Johnny's wife, Mary Syms Harris, who inherited one-half the restaurant, should remarry after his death. The other one-half interest in Johnny Harris Restaurant was bequeathed to Harris's sister, Mary Virginia Harris Bowman of Petersburg, Virginia. In his will, Harris also remembered John Moore, "my trusted colored employee" who helped create the original barbecue sauce recipe.

At the time of Harris's death, his young wife was 30 years old. Despite this restriction in Johnny's will, Mary remarried in 1943, and Red Donaldson was granted one-half interest in the restaurant.

In 1955, Mrs. Bowman and her children sold their half interest in the Johnny Harris Restaurant to Red Donaldson, giving him full ownership of the restaurant he had managed for more than two decades.

The business continued to grow steadily through the decades after Johnny Harris's death, due to a combination of fine food and the congeniality of Red Donaldson. It was a common sight to see him greeting customers himself most nights and weekends. In later years the restaurant truly became a family affair as Red's wife and children were often seen working by his side as his children grew into adulthood.

Johnny Harris's food would not be complete without its famous Bar-B-Cue sauce. Much of the restaurant's reputation was built on this successful sauce, which, like most good Southern barbecue, achieved its distinctive flavor through trial and error over a period of time. When John Moore cooked the sauce recipe for Johnny Harris and produced it in large vats in the back kitchen of the restaurant, requests for the sauce grew, and loyal fans asked for samples to purchase for home use. These samples were bottled in sterilized empty soda bottles. Demand soon surpassed the production capabilities of the busy restaurant kitchen, and in 1950, the official Johnny Harris Famous Bar-B-Cue Sauce Company was founded in a small building across the street from the restaurant. The sauce was, and still is, found on every table in every booth. Over the years specialty flavors of the sauce were created, one of the first being a hickory flavor.

In April of 1959, due to illness, Donaldson regrettably decided to lease out the restaurant. During the two years that he did not operate Johnny Harris, he concentrated on growing the sauce company. As Red aged, he realized that the likely candidate to eventually continue the tradition of the famous restaurant and its sauce was his son Phillip. At age seven, Phillip began to learn the business at his father's knee, where his first duties included picking up cans in the parking lot after busy nights.

After graduating from the University of Georgia in 1957 with a degree in business, Phil left for a three-year stint in the Air Force, where he honed his restaurant skills by managing the officers' club at Davis Monthan Air Force Base in Tucson,

Arizona. He met and married his bride there, and together they returned to Savannah to help with the sauce business.

In 1962, an office area and warehouse were added to the sauce company to store the more than 400 cases being shipped every two weeks. As the cases accumulated, Phil would load up the back of his 1959 Ford station wagon for distribution to the local grocery markets.

Since 1959, the market and sauce production operations have become a full-time

enterprise. Subsequently, the little sauce company has been enlarged to accommodate a growing family of new products. These new offerings include Steak Sauce, Honey Bar-B-Cue Hot Wing Sauce, and Carolina Style Mustard Bar-B-Cue Sauce. These make up the bulk of the sales. In 2011, another group of sauce flavors was developed to include Asian Spice, Mandarin Orange, Pineapple, and Georgia Peach. Other products are the Bar-B-Cue Dry Rub and Shrimp and Crab Boil seasonings.

Top: Red Donaldson greets a bowling team in Savannah that the restaurant sponsored; bottom: Red Donaldson and Buster White, a promoter for this boxing team, shows a Johnny Harris steak to the fighters.

The original flavor of sauce has developed a large following, and all the products are shipped worldwide— especially around the holidays. Numerous appearances on the Food Network and Style Channel have brought call-in orders for days after the restaurant and its sauce are featured.

Kermit Lynnwood "Red" Donaldson died on May 13, 1969, at age 60 in Statesboro, Georgia, after suffering a fatal heart attack at the family farm in Brooklet, Georgia. After Red passed away, his wife Maude took the helm at the restaurant, arriving early each morning to open up and staying until after the lunch rush.

In addition to managing the sauce company, Red's son Phil assumed the role of manager of the restaurant with his brother-in-law, Norman Heidt, as assistant. Norman then developed the catering side of the restaurant into a major enterprise, serving as few as ten guests at a business lunch to as many as 10,000 people when President Carter campaigned through Savannah.

In 2003, the restaurant purchased the adjoining property on Victory Drive and turned it into a banquet facility. It is booked weekly by large tour groups and is also used by various clubs and organizations for monthly meetings. It is always a popular venue for receptions and family reunions.

Joey Hewitt, whose grandfather served as a waiter in the 1960s, chops barbecue meat in the kitchen, always with a winning smile for customers.

In the many years of operating the restaurant, the family has seen many celebrities, sports heroes, and political figures dine under the stars. Their famous autographs can be seen on the covers of hundreds of old menus mounted on the walls in the back hallway, affectionately known as the "hall of fame."

While many new and trendy restaurants have come and gone, Johnny Harris still remains as a testament to its loyal following. Many of the older patrons fondly remember the years long ago when they were dancing and courting at Johnny Harris. Now their children and grandchildren have joined the faithful following. Upon entering the front doors, the unique design and air of nostalgia beckon

The Johnny Harris Restaurant family, left to right: Tracey Heidt Peterson, Corbin Parker (Julie's son), Yvonne Donaldson, Philip Donaldson, Linda Donaldson Heidt, Norman Heidt, Julie Donaldson Lowenthal, and B. J. Lowenthal, Jr. (not pictured: Christen Parker (Corbin's wife) and John K. "Johnny" Donaldson).

tourists and locals alike. On busy weekend nights you can almost imagine the sounds of the big bands that once played here and envision the handsome young men with their elegant ladies dancing under the twinkling lights.

Red Donaldson's smile may have long since faded away, but his legacy still lives on in the hearts and memories of his family and friends. Red's son Phil, son-in-law Norman Heidt, granddaughters Tracey and Julie, along with Julie's husband B.J. and son Corbin, all take an active role in the restaurant today.

In April 2014, the Johnny Harris Restaurant celebrates its 90th birthday. It is one of the oldest (if not *the* oldest) continually operating restaurants in Georgia. Johnny Harris would indeed be very proud to know that the Savannah institution he founded in

1924 during the Roaring Twenties survived the Great Depression, prospered and grew in the capable hands of his good friend Red Donaldson during the dark years of WWII and beyond, and is still a successful family-run and family-friendly restaurant today.

Note from the Author

Johnny Harris Restaurant was a part of my family from the day I was born. I remember Dad leaving before sunrise to make sauce when I was growing up. Then later in the week his station wagon would be full as he delivered the many cases to the local grocery stores. You could always find our family at the restaurant—my grandfather racing around to greet customers, my grandmother working behind the cash register, Dad bouncing between the sauce company and the dining room to oversee daily operations, and my Uncle Norman overseeing the catering business. Almost 20 years ago my husband joined the company, and most recently my son Corbin enjoyed a stint as general manager. Johnny Harris is synonymous with family to me, and so it seemed only fitting that I should tell the story of one of the oldest continuously operating restaurants in Georgia, and the first supper club in Savannah.

For this book, I have gathered the history of the founder, John Newman "Johnny" Harris, as well as his successor, my grandfather, Kermit Lynnwood "Red" Donaldson. Johnny Harris Restaurant has been and continues to be a special gathering place for many locals and visitors. Cherished family memories of engagements, anniversaries, birthday and holiday celebrations at Johnny Harris are passed down through generations. As I began to collect these stories, I realized just how many of these wonderful memories our customers have. I wish they could have all been included in this book, but we had to leave some room for the recipes!

Many of the recipes in this book are now or have been served at the restaurant over the years. Some are old favorites, while others have been seasonal specials, or holiday offerings. Still others have held a special place on our own family table. We hope you enjoy this cookbook, and that the recipes will inspire you to create your own Johnny Harris favorites.

Drinks

Savannah Sweet Tea

serves 8

2 cups sugar
3 family-size tea bags

Pour the sugar into a large pitcher.
Bring ½ gallon water to boil in a large pot. When the water begins to boil, turn off the heat and steep the teabags in the water for 10 minutes. Remove the teabags, bring the brewed tea to a boil, then pour into the pitcher over the sugar and stir until the sugar dissolves. Add a tray of ice cubes and stir until the ice is almost melted, then fill the pitcher up with water.

Savannah Peach Sweet Tea

makes 1 drink

1½ ounces sweet tea vodka
1½ ounces peach schnapps
⅓ cup sweetened or unsweet tea
2 tablespoons lemonade
1 peach, sliced, for garnish

Add the sweet tea vodka and the peach schnapps to a mason jar. Fill with several ice cubes and the sweet or unsweet tea. (The peach schnapps is very sweet, so some people may prefer to use the unsweet tea.) Add a splash of lemonade, garnish with peach slices, and serve.

Johnny Harris Classic Margarita

yields 1 drink

2 ounces tequila, your choice brand
1 ounce Triple Sec, or Gran Marnier
4 ounces sour mix, your choice brand
2 tablespoons orange juice
2 tablespoons Sprite

Pour the tequila and Triple Sec into a cocktail glass, stir in the sour mix, and finish with a splash of orange juice and Sprite. Serve straight up or over ice.

CC's Irish Coffee

yields 1 drink

Hot, strong coffee
2 ounces Jameson Irish whiskey
1 teaspoon brown sugar
Whipped cream
Green crème de menthe
Chocolate syrup

Fill a coffee mug with hot, strong coffee to within 2 inches of the top. Add the Irish whiskey and brown sugar and stir. Top with the whipped cream and drizzle the crème de menthe and chocolate syrup over the top. Serve hot.

1651 EAST
VICTORY DRIVE
SAVANNAH, GEORGIA

TELEPHONE 8290

CORKAGE
CHARGE
ON
ALL BEVERAGES
BROUGHT
INTO THIS BUILDING

MINIMUM
CHECK CHARGE

50c
PER PERSON

•

1936
Souvenir Menu

•

· mɛnu ·
JOHnny HARRIS'

OPENED
SEPTEMBER, 1936

Chatham Artillery Punch (Johnny Harris Version)

1 cup sweet tea
1 quart white zinfandel wine
1 ½ cups orange juice
1 cup light rum
1 cup gin
1 cup blended rye whiskey
1 cup brandy
1 cup sour mix
2 lemons, sliced in thin wedges
1 orange, sliced in thin wedges
4 cups maraschino cherries, with the juice
1 bottle Champagne

In a large punch bowl, add the first 8 ingredients and mix well. Add the lemons, oranges, cherries, and the cherry juice. Fill each glass with ice, ladle the punch into each glass, and top with ¼ cup Champagne.

Bar-B-Cue Bloody Mary

makes 1 drink

1 lime, cut into wedges
¼ cup Johnny Harris Bar-B-Cue Rub, or
  BBQ Dry Rub, see recipe, p. 139
1½ ounces vodka
1 ounce Johnny Harris Bar-B-Cue Sauce, or
  BBQ Sauce, see recipe, p. 136

¾ cup tomato vegetable juice
½ teaspoon Worcestershire sauce
1 celery stick
2 olives

Rub the rim of a cocktail glass with a lime wedge. Spread the barbecue rub mix into a shallow plate and dip the rim of the glass in the rub to coat. Fill the glass with ice.

In a cocktail shaker, combine the vodka, the barbecue sauce, tomato vegetable juice, and the Worcestershire sauce. (You may substitute your favorite bloody mary mix instead of the juice and Worcestershire sauce.) Fill with ice, cover, and shake well. Strain into the prepared glass filled with ice. Garnish with a celery stick, olives, and a lime wedge.

 **RECOLLECTIONS**

During the 1980s, it seemed that a customer named Jim came and ate lunch here every day. He always ordered two Manhattans, except on Saturday when he drank beer. He didn't work on the weekends. He was such a friendly, regular customer that we named a booth after him.

We called him "the bug man" because he owned an exterminating company here in Savannah.

When he died, we put a plaque on the windowsill in the Kitchen dining room at his booth. It is the last booth by the door.

Above, a view of the old bar at the original Johnny Harris Tavern. Currently, the Tavern room, below, is located at the back of the restaurant. Oppositge, the Hall of Fame—so-named for the many celebrity-autographed menus that hang on the wall—leads into the Tavern.

Southern Lady

makes 1 drink

1 ounce American Harvest Vodka
1 ounce peach schnapps
1 ounce pomegranate liqueur
2 ounces pineapple juice
2 ounces cranberry juice
1 ounce lemon-lime soda, or Sprite

In a cocktail shaker, mix the first 5 ingredients and pour into a tall glass. Add the desired amount of ice, then top the glass off with lemon-lime soda, or Sprite.

Old Fashioned Lemonade

serves 8

2 cups sugar
1½ cups fresh squeezed lemon juice
  (6 medium-size lemons)
2 lemons, thinly sliced, for garnish
3 to 4 fresh mint sprigs, for garnish

Heat the sugar with 1 cup water in a medium saucepan over medium-high heat and bring to a boil, stirring until the sugar is dissolved. Pour the sugar syrup into a large pitcher, add the lemon juice and 8 cups water. Stir well and add the lemon slices. Serve over ice and garnish with sprigs of mint.

Whisky Sour

serves 4

2 cups fresh orange juice
½ cup lemon juice
⅓ cup fine sugar
1 cup bourbon, your choice brand

Fill a drink pitcher halfway full of ice. Add all the ingredients and stir well to blend.

Black and Blue Martini

makes 1 drink

1½ ounces Three Olives Cherry Vodka
1 ounce raspberry liqueur, Razzmatazz or your choice
½ ounce Blue Curacao
1 ounce sour mix
1 ounce soda, optional
1 orange slice

Add the first 4 ingredients to a cocktail shaker. (You may want to add the soda to cut the sweetness a bit.) Fill with ice and shake well. Strain into a martini glass and garnish with an orange slice.

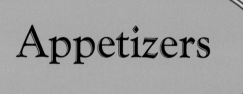

Appetizers

Fried Green Tomatoes
with Homemade Pimento Cheese

serves 6 to 8 / yields 2½ cups pimento cheese

Thinner tomato slices become crisp, while thicker slices tend to remain juicy in the center when they are fried. We make them on the juicy side at the restaurant.

4 large green tomatoes, sliced ¼- to
  ½-inch thick
1½ cup buttermilk
1 teaspoon salt
1 teaspoon pepper
1 cup all-purpose flour
1 cup self-rising cornmeal
3 cups vegetable oil

Homemade Pimento Cheese
½ pound extra sharp Vermont cheddar
  cheese, grated
½ pound mild cheddar cheese, grated
1 (7-ounce) jar pimentos, drained, and
  chopped into ¼-inch pieces
½ teaspoon cayenne pepper
Salt to taste
1 cup mayonnaise

Place the tomato slices in a large shallow dish. Pour the buttermilk over the tomatoes and turn to coat each piece. Sprinkle with salt and pepper.

Combine the flour and cornmeal in a separate shallow dish or pie plate, then dredge each slice of tomato in the flour mixture.

In a large heavy skillet, heat the oil over medium heat until a small drop of batter dropped into the oil sizzles. Fry the tomato slices in batches for 3 minutes on each side, or until golden brown. Drain the fried tomatoes on paper towels and sprinkle lightly with salt to taste.

To make the pimento cheese: Place both cheeses into a large mixing bowl and add the chopped pimentos, cayenne pepper, salt, and mayonnaise. Using a fork, mix the ingredients well and then mash until all the cheese is well moistened. You may add more mayonnaise if you wish. Any remaining pimento cheese may be stored in a sealed dish in the refrigerator for up to 1 week.

Place 2 to 3 fried green tomatoes on each plate and serve with a large dollop of pimento cheese.

Baked Vidalia Onion Dip

yields 2 cups

These large sweet onions are grown in south Georgia, but any sweet mild onion will do. Serve these dips with your favorite crackers, chips, and vegetable slices.

1 large Vidalia or sweet onion, finely chopped
1 cup grated Swiss cheese
1 cup mayonnaise
1 clove garlic, minced
1 teaspoon hot pepper sauce
½ cup grated Parmesan cheese

Preheat the oven to 375 degrees F.

Combine the first 5 ingredients in a medium bowl and mix well. Transfer the dip to a shallow baking dish, sprinkle the top evenly with the Parmesan cheese, and bake for 25 minutes, until the edges are bubbly and the top is golden brown.

Skidaway Crab Dip

serves 8 to 10

2 (8-ounce) packages cream cheese, softened
1½ pounds lump crab meat
1 cup sour cream
½ stick butter
½ cup mayonnaise
1 small Vidalia or sweet onion, finely chopped
½ cup coarsely grated sharp cheddar cheese
¼ cup red bell pepper, finely chopped
1 teaspoon Worcestershire sauce
2 tablespoons lemon juice
2 teaspoons hot pepper sauce
2 cloves garlic, minced
½ cup Panko bread crumbs
½ cup Parmesan cheese, finely grated

Preheat the oven to 350 degrees F.

Melt the cream cheese in a medium saucepan over low heat. Add the remaining ingredients, except for the Panko and Parmesan cheese, and mix gently, taking care not to break up the crabmeat. Spread the mixture evenly in a 2-quart baking dish. Mix the Panko with the Parmesan cheese and sprinkle evenly over the top of the crabmeat mixture. Bake for 20 to 25 minutes until hot and bubbly.

Maple Room Tavern Spinach Dip

serves 8 to 10

This version of a spinach dip gets a little color from the tomatoes and a little kick from the green chilies.

1 medium Vidalia or sweet onion, chopped
1 plum tomato, finely chopped
1 (4-ounce) can green chilies, drained and chopped
2 cloves garlic, minced
2 (10-ounce) frozen spinach, thawed and drained
1 (8-ounce) package cream cheese, room temperature

10 ounces grated Monterey Jack cheese
1 cup half-and-half
1 tablespoon red wine vinegar
Salt and pepper to taste
2 tablespoons sour cream
Tortilla chips

Preheat the oven to 400 degrees F.
In a medium skillet, sauté the onion over medium heat for 3 to 4 minutes until softened. Add the tomatoes, chilies, and garlic and cook for 2 minutes. Transfer to a large bowl and stir in the spinach, cream cheese, Monterey Jack cheese, half-and-half, and vinegar, and season with salt and pepper. Spoon the mixture into a shallow baking dish and bake 30 to 35 minutes, or until the dip is light brown and bubbly. Top with the sour cream and serve with tortilla chips.

Crab and Grilled Corn Dip

yields 3 cups

This recipe can also be made with frozen corn kernels, but you will miss the slight smokey taste that fresh corn hot off the grill imparts.

3 ears fresh yellow corn
8 ounces cream cheese, softened
¼ cup chopped scallions
¼ cup mayonnaise

3 tablespoons freshly squeezed lemon juice
2 teaspoons seafood seasoning
6 ounces lump crabmeat, picked clean of shells

Preheat the oven to 350 degrees F.

Place the fresh corn, still in the husks, directly on a medium-hot grill for 10 to 15 minutes, until the kernels are tender. Let cool enough to remove the husks, then place the cobs directly on the grill to lightly char for 1 to 2 minutes, turning to char evenly. Cut the kernels from the cobs and place in a medium bowl. Gently fold in the cream cheese, scallions, mayonnaise, lemon juice, seafood seasoning, and crabmeat and spread the dip in a baking dish. Cover with aluminum foil and bake for 40 to 45 minutes until the dish is heated through and bubbly around the edges.

Sweet Potato Corn and Cheddar Fritters

yields 14 fritters

2 large sweet potatoes, boiled until tender
1 green onion, diced
1 cup corn kernels, fresh or frozen
3 tablespoons yellow corn meal
2 tablespoons brown sugar
½ cup cheddar cheese, coarsely grated

½ teaspoon paprika
Salt and pepper to taste
¾ cup Panko breadcrumbs
Vegetable oil for frying
Honey Mustard Sauce, see recipe p. 138

Peel the boiled sweet potatoes and mash them in a large bowl until smooth. Add the onions, corn, cornmeal, brown sugar, cheese, paprika, salt, and pepper and continue mixing to fully combine all the ingredients.

Roll 2 tablespoons of the mixture into a ball and place it on a shallow platter. Continue until all the mixture is used. Refrigerate the balls for 15 to 20 minutes to firm them up.

In the meantime, pour oil into a medium skillet to a depth of ½-inch and heat the oil over medium heat. Place the Panko in a zip-top bag and drop the chilled balls in the bag, one at a time, rolling them until they are fully coated.

Once the oil has reached frying temperature (a drop of water will sizzle when dropped into the oil), fry a third of the balls at a time for 2 minutes per side, turning, until golden brown. Remove them with a slotted spoon and drain on paper towels. Serve the fritters warm with a drizzle of honey mustard sauce.

Low Country Baked Shrimp

serves 6 to 8

2 pounds fresh medium shrimp, shelled and deveined

1 tablespoon minced Vidalia or sweet onion

2 cloves garlic, minced

3 tablespoons butter, melted

1 tablespoon Worcestershire sauce

1 tablespoon fresh lemon juice

1 tablespoon seafood seasoning

1 teaspoon paprika

1 teaspoon hot pepper sauce

Salt and pepper to taste

Preheat the oven to 325 degrees F.

In a large bowl, combine the shrimp, onions, and the garlic, and toss well. Add the remaining ingredients and toss until the shrimp are well coated. Using a pair of tongs, arrange the shrimp in a single layer in a large, shallow baking dish, or an oven-safe skillet, and bake for 10 minutes. Turn the shrimp over and continue to bake for 10 more minutes until the shrimp turn pink.

Transfer the shrimp to a large serving platter and serve hot.

RECOLLECTIONS

In the early days of the restaurant, waiters didn't write down orders. We had no electronic method of creating a check. Instead, we had Nellie Harrod, who was our food checker. Waiters would pick up their orders in the kitchen and bring their trays of food to Nellie on the way to the table. Nellie would ring up the total, like at a grocery store.

All the waiters were scared of her. We had three different sizes of T-bones on the menu, and waiters would race through Nellie's station with a large T-bone on the platter, hoping she wouldn't notice the size and charge for a smaller one. That way, they figured they could do their favorite customers a favor and get a bigger tip. She was checker during the '40s and '50s, and we kept up the practice of using food checkers through the 1970s. –Norman Heidt

White Bean Bruschetta

yields about 20

1 cup Great Northern beans, cooked
3 plum tomatoes, seeded and chopped
¼ cup chopped, pitted Greek olives
6 tablespoons olive oil
¼ cup fresh basil, chopped

1 tablespoon minced garlic
Salt and pepper to taste
1 baguette, sliced ⅓-inch thick
1 (5.3-ounce) package goat cheese

In a large bowl, combine the beans, tomatoes, olives, 4 tablespoons oil, the basil, garlic, salt, and pepper, and set aside.

Place the bread slices on an ungreased baking sheet and brush the tops with the remaining 2 tablespoons oil. Broil the bread slices on a rack 3 to 4 inches from the heat for 1 to 2 minutes, until golden brown.

Spread each piece of toast with a teaspoon of goat cheese and top with a teaspoon of the bean mixture. Serve immediately.

BBQ, Bacon, and Blue Fries

serves 6 to 8

6 large potatoes, sliced, or 1 large bag frozen
   potato slices
6 cups vegetable oil, for frying
8 strips bacon, fried and crumbled
1 cup blue cheese dressing

1 cup Johnny Harris Bar-B-Cue Sauce, or
   BBQ Sauce, see recipe. p. 136
½ cup blue cheese crumbles

If you are using fresh potatoes, slice the potatoes into ½-inch thick strips.

Fill a deep fryer with 6 cups vegetable oil and heat to 375 degrees F.

Fry the potatoes in batches for 5 to 6 minutes, until golden brown. Use a slotted spoon or tongs to remove the fries, and drain on paper towels.

Place the hot potatoes in a mound on a large serving platter. Drizzle the blue cheese dressing evenly over the top, followed by the barbecue sauce. Top with the bacon bits and blue cheese crumbles, and serve hot.

Harris's Crab and Spinach Au Gratin

serves 6 to 8

1 ½ pounds fresh baby spinach leaves, rinsed and chopped
⅓ cup butter
1 pound lump crabmeat, picked clean of shells
1 clove garlic, minced
1 tablespoon all-purpose flour
1 ½ cups (6 ounces) grated Monterey Jack cheese

8 ounces cream cheese, softened
1 cup half-and-half
1 teaspoon salt
½ teaspoon white pepper
¼ teaspoon ground cayenne pepper
¾ cup cheddar cheese, shredded

Preheat the oven to 350 F.

Bring a large saucepan of water to boil over medium-high heat. Boil the spinach until it is bright green and wilted, then drain and set aside.

Melt the butter in a medium skillet over medium heat and sauté the crabmeat and garlic for 3 minutes, stirring gently so not to break up the large lumps of crabmeat. Remove the crabmeat mixture to a bowl and stir the flour into the same skillet, blending well. Add the Monterey Jack and cream cheese to the skillet and continue stirring over low heat until the cheeses are melted and well-combined. Add the half-and-half, the salt, and both peppers and continue cooking over medium heat, until the sauce is hot and bubbly.

Remove from heat and gently fold the spinach and crabmeat into the cheese sauce. Pour into a shallow 9 x 12-inch casserole dish, sprinkle the top with cheddar cheese and bake for 10 minutes.

Crab-Stuffed Mushrooms

yields 2 dozen

1 cup fresh crabmeat, finely chopped
½ cup cream cheese, softened
1 cup grated Monterey Jack cheese
3 cloves garlic, minced
2 teaspoons melted butter
24 large, fresh mushrooms, cleaned and
   stems removed

Preheat the oven to 400 degrees F.

Mix the crabmeat, cream cheese, Monterey Jack cheese, and garlic together in a bowl.

Dip the mushrooms into the melted butter and place each one in a cup of two 12-cup muffin tins, bottom side up, to form a cup. Fill the mushrooms with a spoonful of the crabmeat mixture and bake for 15 minutes.

 **RECOLLECTIONS**

Johnny Harris Restaurant has hosted its fair share of celebrity diners, as evidenced by the scores of framed, autographed menus hanging in its hallways. We have also catered events for celebrities, and one that stands out in my mind was in 1978 when then-President Jimmy Carter was the featured speaker at the Hibernian Banquet, an annual event that takes place the evening of St. Patrick's Day and is hosted by the 180-year-old Savannah Irish organization, the Hibernian Society.

The event was held at the downtown Civic Center, and Secret Service men had arranged the schedule that evening for security reasons. Carter was expected to arrive after the dinner, just before he was to speak. That way, the waiters—who had not received security clearance for the event—could serve the dinners, since the President wouldn't be in the building yet. Unfortunately for the guests, Carter showed up early, so the floor had to be cleared of waiters.

All that great Johnny Harris food went to waste that night! –Norman Heidt

Fried Asparagus

serves 6 to 8

I'm not sure who came up with the idea to fry asparagus, but it has been on the Johnny Harris menu as long as I can remember. And once I tried it, I was hooked! You will be, too. It's a great way to get kids to eat their vegetables.

½ cup all-purpose flour
½ cup light yellow cornmeal
1¼ teaspoons baking powder
1 teaspoon salt
¾ teaspoon baking soda
¾ teaspoon garlic salt
½ teaspoon fresh ground pepper

1 cup beer
3 egg whites
Vegetable oil, for frying
2½ pounds thin fresh asparagus, trimmed
Ranch dressing, or horseradish sauce

To make the batter, combine the first seven ingredients in a large bowl.

In a smaller bowl, combine the beer and egg whites, then slowly stir these into the dry ingredients until the batter is just moistened.

Fill an electric skillet with vegetable oil to a depth of 1½ inches and heat to 375 degrees F. Using a fork, dip each asparagus spear into the batter to coat, gently place it into the hot oil, and fry for 2 to 3 minutes on each side until golden brown. Drain the cooked asparagus on paper towels and serve immediately with Ranch dressing or horseradish sauce (see recipe, p. 139) for dipping.

 **RECOLLECTIONS**

Before and after WWII, Johnny Harris was the foremost dinner club in the city, along with The Rex, Johnny Ganem, and The Sapphire Room at the De Soto Hotel. People stood in line to get in and dance to jazz and big band orchestra music until the early morning hours. It was considered bad taste if you didn't wear a coat and tie—in fact, a customer couldn't get into the main dining room without them. We kept a collection of men's coats in various sizes to lend people who didn't wear one. This practice continued until the 1980s.

–Philip Donaldson

Bacon-Wrapped Jalapeño Bundles

yields 2 dozen

12 fresh jalapeños
1 (8-ounce) package cream cheese, softened
2 teaspoons garlic powder
12 strips center-cut bacon

Preheat the oven to 400 degrees F.

Wash the jalapeños, remove the stems, slice in half lengthwise, and discard the seeds.

Mix together the softened cream cheese and the garlic powder. Fill each jalapeño half with the cream cheese mixture.

Cut the bacon strips in half, and wrap each stuffed jalapeño half with the bacon. Place the bundles on a baking sheet lined with foil and bake for 30 minutes, or until the bacon is thoroughly cooked. The bacon will look bright red when the bundles are done.

 **RECOLLECTIONS**

Johnny Mercer, the award-winning songwriter and composer, and a native of Savannah, ate often at Johnny Harris, preferring to sit in the Kitchen instead of the Grand Ballroom. He spent most of his time in New York or Los Angeles when he was working, but when he was in town he loved to come eat fried chicken and barbecue sauce. He even sent some Original Johnny Harris Sauce to Maudie Chasen, of the famous Chasen's Restaurant in Beverly Hills, as a gift.

Mercer liked to tell people that the bartender at Johnny Harris was the only man who knew a reliable cure for hiccups. He also mentioned in a radio interview that every city should have a restaurant like Johnny Harris. —Norman Heidt

Buffalo Chicken Dip

serves 6 to 8

1 (8-ounce) package cream cheese
½ cup blue cheese salad dressing
½ cup Johnny Harris Hot Wing Sauce, or
   Spicy Honey BBQ Sauce. see recipe, p. 137
½ cup crumbled blue cheese, or shredded
   mozzarella cheese
2 cups shredded cooked chicken

Preheat the oven to 350 degrees F.

Microwave the cream cheese in a medium microwave-safe bowl on high for 1 minute to soften. Whisk the salad dressing, buffalo wing sauce, and the blue cheese together with the cream cheese until smooth. Stir in the shredded chicken until the sauce thoroughly coats the meat.

Spread the chicken mixture into a 9-inch, deep-dish pie plate and bake for 20 minutes until the mixture is heated through. Remove from the oven and stir well.

Serve with crackers, celery sticks, or vegetable slices. This dip also works well in a fondue pot or small crock.

Soups

Bacon, Corn, and Shrimp Chowder

serves 8 to 10

1 package sliced bacon, chopped
2 large Vidalia or sweet onions, chopped
1 cup chopped celery
1 1/2 teaspoons chopped fresh thyme
2 garlic cloves, minced
8 cups fresh or frozen corn kernels
4 cups chicken broth
1 1/2 pounds medium shrimp, peeled and
    deveined
2 cups half-and-half
1 teaspoon Johnny Harris Seafood
    Seasoning, or Seafood Seasoning, see
    recipe, p. 138
1/2 teaspoon salt
1/2 teaspoon coarse ground pepper

In a large Dutch oven over medium high heat, sauté the bacon for 4 minutes, or until it begins to brown. Drain 1/3 of the bacon on paper towels, leaving the rest in the pot. Add the onions, celery, thyme, and garlic to the pot and sauté for 3 minutes. Add the corn and cook 2 more minutes, stirring occasionally. Add the chicken broth and bring to a boil. Turn the heat down slightly, and cook for 5 minutes.

Scoop 4 cups of the corn mixture out of the pot and place in a blender. (Make sure you remove the center piece of the blender to allow the steam to escape. You will want to cover this with a towel to avoid splatters.) Blend the corn mixture until smooth, and then return the puree to the pot. Stir in the shrimp and cook 2 to 3 minutes or until the shrimp turn pink. Stir in the half-and–half, the seafood seasoning, salt, and pepper.

Ladle the soup into individual bowls and crumble the reserved bacon over the top of each serving.

She Crab Soup

serves 6 to 8

This soup has been on the menu for over 40 years and is a favorite of many. The consistency can be thinned according to personal taste by adding more cream, or thickened by adding more flour. The fish stock adds rich flavor and depth to the soup.

1 quart heavy cream
⅛ teaspoon salt
⅛ teaspoon pepper
¼ cup unsalted butter
⅓ cup all-purpose flour
2 cups hot fish stock, see recipe
2 tablespoons lemon juice
¼ teaspoon ground nutmeg
1 pound fresh crabmeat, picked clean
    for shells
⅓ cup good quality sherry
Chopped parsley, for garnish

Fish Stock
2 tablespoons olive oil
2 shallots, coarsely chopped
1 head garlic, sliced in half
½ cup fennel stalks, chopped
4 black peppercorns
1 carrot, coarsely chopped
Fish bones of 1 to 2 lean, white-fleshed
    fish (halibut or flounder), coarsely
    chopped
½ cup white wine

Combine the first 3 ingredients in a heavy saucepan and bring them to a boil over medium heat. Reduce the heat and simmer for 1 hour, stirring occasionally.

Meanwhile, make the fish stock. Heat the olive oil in a saucepan over medium heat and add the shallots, garlic halves, fennel, peppercorns, and carrot, and sauté for 3 to 4 minutes. Add the fish bones and sauté for another 5 to 7 minutes before stirring in the wine and 2½ cups water. Heat until the stock just starts to bubble around the edges of the pan, then reduce the heat to low and simmer for 20 minutes. Pour the stock through a strainer, and discard the vegetables and bones. Use immediately or cover and refrigerate until ready to use. (This stock may also be frozen in ½-cup portions indefinitely.)

Melt the butter in a separate large heavy saucepan over low heat. Gradually add the flour and stir until smooth. Cook for 1 minute, stirring constantly. Gradually add the fish stock and continue cooking over medium heat for 3 minutes, until thickened. Stir in the cream mixture and continue to cook just until thoroughly heated. Add in the lemon juice, nutmeg, and crabmeat and stir until all ingredients are thoroughly incorporated.

Top each bowl of soup with 1 to 2 teaspoons sherry, if desired, and sprinkle with chopped parsley. (Note: Please use a good quality sherry and not cooking sherry for this soup.)

Low Country Shrimp Chowder

serves 10 to 12

1 teaspoon salt
6 cups fresh or frozen yellow corn kernels
¼ cup unsalted butter
2 large sweet onions, finely chopped
½ cup all-purpose flour
1 teaspoon black pepper
1 teaspoon Johnny Harris Seafood Seasoning

10 cups chicken broth
1½ pounds potatoes, peeled and chopped
1 cup half-and-half
½ pound sharp cheddar cheese, coarsely shredded
1½ pounds shrimp, peeled and deveined

Fill a medium saucepan half full of water, add the salt, and bring to a boil over high heat. Add the corn and cook over high heat for 3 minutes. Drain the corn in a colander, rinse under cold water, and set aside.

Melt the butter in a medium Dutch oven over medium-high heat and sauté the onions for 6 to 8 minutes, or until they are tender and translucent in color. Stir in the flour, pepper, and seafood seasoning and continue to cook, stirring, for 3 minutes. Add the chicken broth and potatoes, bring the pot to a boil, and cook for 20 to 25 minutes, or until the potatoes are fork-tender. Lower the heat to medium and stir in the corn, half-and-half, cheese, and shrimp and cook for an 3 additional minutes until the shrimp are pink. Serve immediately.

 **RECOLLECTIONS**

Ray Capers was a part-time barbecue cook back in the 1940s. He became known as the world's fastest chicken-plucker. He had a 55 gallon drum of boiling water that he used to loosen the feathers. Word got around about this and Mr. Ripley, who wrote a column called "Ripley's Believe It Or Not" that was very popular at the time, came to Savannah to see for himself just how fast Ray could pluck chickens. He wrote an article about Ray in 1946 claiming that Ray could pluck 1700 chickens in an 8-hour work day!

We keep Ray's picture up in the restaurant. –Philip Donaldson

Vidalia Onion Soup

serves 8

The Vidalia onion, discovered in the early 1930s, is a sweet onion grown in the southeastern region of Georgia around the city of Vidalia. Vidalia onions are grown in 13 counties and portions of 7 others. They have a mild, sweet flavor due to the lack of sulfur in the soil of this region and are used in many recipes in Georgia and the Southeast. This soup is a perfect recipe to showcase their mild sweet flavor.

2 tablespoons olive oil
4 large Vidalia onions, sliced
4 cloves garlic, minced
¾ cup dry sherry
7 cups chicken broth
1 tablespoon fresh thyme

1 bay leaf
1 teaspoon hot pepper sauce
1 loaf French bread, cut diagonally
    into 1-inch slices and toasted
8 to 12 slices provolone cheese

In a large stockpot over medium heat, heat the olive oil, add the onions, and cook, stirring occasionally, for 20 minutes. Add the garlic and continue to cook for 10 more minutes. When the onions are a light caramel color, add the sherry and cook until the liquid has almost evaporated. Stir in the chicken broth, thyme, bay leaf, and hot pepper sauce. Bring the mixture to a boil, then reduce the heat to low, and cover. Let the soup simmer for 15 to 20 minutes, then remove the bay leaf.

Preheat the oven to 400 degrees F.

Ladle the soup into ovenproof bowls and top with a toasted bread slice and 1 to 2 slices provolone cheese. Place the bowls on a baking sheet and bake 5 minutes until the cheese has melted and is bubbly.

Lentil Soup

serves 8 to 10

2 tablespoons olive oil
1 Vidalia or sweet onion, chopped
3 carrots, finely chopped
2 cloves garlic, minced
2 (32-ounce) cartons vegetable broth
1 pound lentils, rinsed and drained

¼ cup tomato paste
¼ cup Johnny Harris Steak Sauce or Steak
  Sauce, see recipe p. 137
1 teaspoon dried thyme
1 teaspoon ground black pepper
6 cups baby spinach leaves

In a large Dutch oven, heat the olive oil over medium-high heat, then add the onions, carrots, and garlic and cook, stirring frequently, for 6 to 8 minutes, until the vegetables are slightly tender. Stir in the vegetable broth, lentils, tomato paste, the steak sauce, thyme, and pepper. Cover the pot and bring the mixture to a boil over high heat. Then reduce the heat to low and simmer for another 40 minutes.

Stir in the spinach and simmer, uncovered, for 10 minutes or until the lentils are tender.

Black-Eyed Pea Soup

serves 8

3 to 4 slices bacon
2 tablespoons olive oil
2 cups finely chopped Vidalia or sweet onions
1 tablespoon garlic, minced
3 (12-ounce) packages frozen black-eyed peas
  or 6 cups fresh

4 cups chicken broth
2 (8-ounce) cans tomato sauce
1 teaspoon cayenne pepper
1 teaspoon red wine vinegar
Salt and pepper to taste
Freshly grated Parmesan cheese

In a large Dutch oven over medium heat, fry the bacon until crisp, then transfer to paper towels to drain. Add the olive oil to the bacon grease left in the pot, then stir in the onions and garlic and sauté for 5 to 6 minutes, or until the onions are tender. Crumble the bacon into small pieces and add to the pot along with the black-eyed peas, chicken broth, tomato sauce, and cayenne pepper. Simmer for 45 minutes to 1 hour, until the flavors are well blended and the peas are tender. Before serving, stir in the vinegar and season to taste with salt and pepper. Ladle the soup into bowls and sprinkle each serving with Parmesan cheese. Serve immediately.

Cream of Artichoke Soup

serves 6 to 8

6 tablespoons unsalted butter
½ cup finely chopped onion
½ cup finely chopped celery
6 tablespoons all-purpose flour
6 cups chicken broth
¼ cup freshly squeezed lemon juice
1 teaspoon salt
¼ teaspoon ground black pepper

¼ teaspoon thyme
1 (15-ounce) can artichoke quarters,
   drained and chopped
2 cups heavy cream
1 lemon, sliced, for garnish
Sprigs thyme, for garnish

Melt the butter in a large saucepan over medium heat. Add onion and celery and sauté for 6 to 8 minutes, until tender. Add the flour, stirring to coat the vegetables. Add the chicken broth and lemon juice and continue to cook for 3 to 5 minutes, or until the liquid thickens. Season with salt, pepper, and thyme, then add the artichokes, reduce the heat, and simmer for 30 minutes.

Transfer the soup to a food processor or blender in batches, and puree, taking care to vent the lid properly to allow steam to escape. Return the pureed soup to the saucepan and add the cream. Slowly reheat over low heat, being careful not to boil the soup.

Ladle portions into bowls and garnish with lemon slices and fresh thyme.

Baked Potato Soup

serves 6 to 8

2 to 3 tablespoons olive oil
1 medium onion, chopped
⅔ cup all-purpose flour
6 cups chicken broth
5 large Russet potatoes, baked, peeled, and
   thinly sliced
2 cups half-and-half
¼ cup chopped parsley
1½ teaspoons minced garlic

1 teaspoon salt
1 teaspoon pepper
¼ cup chopped green onions
1 cup cheddar cheese, crumbled, plus more
   to garnish
4 slices bacon, cooked crisp, for garnish
Sour cream, for garnish

Heat the olive oil in a large saucepan over medium-high heat and sauté the onion for 3 to 5 minutes, until transparent. Add the flour and stir until the mixture just begins to turn golden. Whisk in the chicken broth until the liquid thickens. Add the potatoes and stir in the half-and-half, parsley, garlic, salt, and pepper. Reduce the heat to low and simmer for 10 minutes, being very careful not to boil. Add the green onions and one cup cheddar cheese, and heat just until the cheese melts. Ladle the soup into bowls and garnish each serving with the bacon, cheddar cheese, and sour cream.

 **RECOLLECTIONS**

In 1995 I joined the family business. My first assignment was manning the dining room. Most people's first day on the job would contain some level of fear of the boss. It didn't take me long to realize who my "real" boss was—the Johnny Harris customers. At one point that day I made eye contact with a guest who summoned me to come over to his table. Upon arrival I was asked, "Who are you?" I responded that I was the new member of the management team. I was then "interviewed" and given a quick lesson on the correct specification of the dish the guest was enjoying. Many Johnny Harris customers began coming here before I was born. I quickly realized that there was a degree of entitlement bestowed upon guests of senior status. The long and short of it is, at Johnny Harris, there is a feeling among many of its patrons that they are the boss and we are the guests—until you survive long enough that they grant you proper tenure to be a real manager. Eighteen years later I'm still working on my tenure! —B.J. Lowenthal, Jr.

Deep South Seafood Stew

serves 8

⅓ cup vegetable oil
1 medium onion, chopped
1 red bell pepper, chopped
2 cloves garlic, minced
3 tablespoons all-purpose flour
4 cups chicken broth
1 (28-ounce) can diced tomatoes, with juice
1 pound cooked lump crabmeat
½ pound fresh okra, cut into ½-inch rounds
2 bay leaves
1 teaspoon dried basil

1 teaspoon dried oregano
1 teaspoon dried thyme
1 teaspoon hot pepper sauce
Salt and pepper to taste
1 pound smoked sausage, sliced in ¼-inch-thick slices
1 pound medium shrimp, peeled and deveined
4 cups long grain white rice, steamed

Heat the oil in a large saucepan over medium heat and sauté the onions and red bell pepper for 6 to 8 minutes until tender. Add the garlic and reduce the heat to low. Stir in the flour and cook for 5 minutes, or until the flour turns slightly brown. Stir in the chicken broth slowly and add the tomatoes with juice, the crabmeat, okra, bay leaves, basil, oregano, thyme, hot pepper sauce, salt and pepper. Bring the mixture to a boil, then reduce the heat and simmer for 1 hour.

  Add the sausage and shrimp and continue to simmer for 5 minutes, or until the shrimp are pink and cooked through. Mound ½ cup steamed rice in the bottom of each bowl and ladle the stew over the rice.

Black Bean Soup

serves 8 to 10

6 slices bacon, chopped
2 cups Vidalia or sweet onion, chopped
4 cloves garlic, minced
4 (15-ounce) cans black beans, drained
3½ cups chicken broth
2 tablespoons tomato paste
½ cup Johnny Harris Steak Sauce, or
   BBQ Sauce, see recipe, p. 136

½ teaspoon salt
2 tablespoons chopped fresh cilantro
½ cup sharp cheddar cheese, coarsely grated
Sour cream, for garnish

In a large Dutch oven over medium-high heat, cook the bacon until crispy. Drain on paper towels. Add the onion and garlic to the bacon drippings in the pan and cook 5 to 6 minutes, stirring occasionally, until the onion is tender. Add the black beans, chicken broth, tomato paste, steak sauce, and salt and bring the mixture to a boil over high heat, then reduce the heat to low and simmer for 20 minutes.

Transfer half the soup to a blender or food processor and puree, taking care to vent the lid properly to allow steam to escape. (You may want to cover the top with a towel to prevent spills or splatters.) Blend until smooth, then stir the puree back into the reserved soup. Stir in the cilantro just before serving.

Ladle the soup into individual bowls and garnish each serving with a sprinkle of cheddar cheese, a teaspoon of sour cream, and additional cilantro as desired.

Chilled Summer Shrimp Soup

serves 8

¼ cup olive oil
1 medium Vidalia or sweet onion, finely
  chopped
2 teaspoons mild curry powder
4 cloves garlic, minced
3 pounds fresh shrimp, peeled and deveined
4 (10-ounce) packages frozen whole kernel
  corn, or 6 cups fresh, cooked

2 cups sour cream
4 cups buttermilk
2 teaspoons salt
3 teaspoons freshly ground black pepper
4 teaspoons hot pepper sauce
4 tablespoons minced chives

Heat the olive oil in a large sauté pan over medium heat. Add the onion, curry powder, and garlic, and cook 5 to 6 minutes until the onion is translucent. Add the shrimp and sauté for 5 minutes, until they turn pink. Remove from the heat and allow the mixture to cool completely.

Combine 4 cups corn, the sour cream, and the buttermilk in a food processor and process in batches until smooth. Transfer each batch of soup to a large storage container fitted with a lid.

Add the remaining corn, the shrimp mixture, salt, pepper, and hot sauce to the storage container and stir well. Cover tightly and refrigerate at least 2 hours.

Serve the cold soup in chilled bowls and sprinkle 1 teaspoon of minced chives atop each serving.

Charlene Shourtall
Server

I started working at Johnny Harris in 1984 and have worked here on and off since then. I worked as a bartender in the 1990s, but I prefer waitressing because it's a hands-on job with the customers.

I have a lot of older clientele that come especially to see me and have me serve them. Some people bring me gifts. One lady brought me material to make a tie, because I make my own ties to wear to work as part of my uniform.

I made the one I'm wearing here, and it was hand-painted by Christen Deloach Parker, Corbin's wife. I've made ties for other waiters, too. I put my name tag on the back of the tie if I give it away.

I also make ties for every holiday—with wineglasses, Easter bunnies, Christmas lights, flags for July Fourth—you name it, I've made it.

Noella Houston
Server

I have been a server at Johnny Harris Restaurant for six years. When I started to work here, they still had bands playing once a month on Saturday nights.

I like people, and a lot of customers ask for me to serve them when they come in. Some come from out of town only once a year to eat here, but they will ask for me personally. I have a lot of "call parties," people who request me. I remember all my customers' favorite things to eat, so they have to tell me right away if they are going to change their orders.

Sometimes I get gifts from customers. I complimented one lady on her beautiful necklace, and the next time she came she had made one for me. I even get Christmas gifts from some of my customers.

I am not bashful—if I'm standing across the room and I see one of my customers come in, I will yell hello to them and call them by name. They like that.

Cream of Chicken Soup

serves 6

4 tablespoons butter
6 shallots, chopped
2 leeks, sliced
3 cups chicken stock
1 tablespoon chopped fresh parsley
1 tablespoon chopped fresh thyme

Salt and freshly ground pepper to taste
1 ½ pounds boneless chicken breasts,
   cooked and finely chopped
1 cup heavy cream
Sprigs thyme, for garnish

Melt the butter in a large pan over medium heat and sauté the shallots for 3 minutes, or until they are slightly softened. Add the leek and cook another 5 minutes, stirring often. Add the stock, parsley, and thyme and season to taste with salt and pepper. Bring to a boil over high heat, then reduce the heat and simmer for 25 minutes. Remove from the heat and let cool for 10 minutes.

Transfer the soup in batches to a food processor, or blender, and process until smooth. Return the soup to a clean saucepan, add the chicken, and warm over low heat for 10 minutes. Stir in the cream and cook for another 2 minutes. Remove from the heat and ladle into bowls. Garnish with sprigs of thyme.

 **RECOLLECTIONS**

During the early 1900s, Estill Avenue, where the original Johnny Harris Tavern and Barbecue Restaurant was located, was just a dirt road. From 1908 to 1911, the first Grand Prix races in the U.S. were held in Savannah. The Vanderbilt Cup was also held here, running in part along Estill Avenue. In 1919, Estill Avenue was paved and renamed Victory Drive. It was planted with grass medians and lined with palms. The name change was a memorial to all the servicemen and women from Chatham County who were killed during WWI. Each Palmetto tree represented a fallen hero.

At the time it was built, it was said to be the "longest Palmetto Palm-lined drive in the world." In the early 1920s, Victory Drive was extended for nearly 18 miles, connecting Savannah to Tybee Island. Many Johnny Harris customers would stop by to get food for their picnics as they headed out of town to Tybee Island beach.

Country Cabbage Soup

serves 10 to 12

2 pounds lean ground beef
2 (28-ounce) cans stewed tomatoes
1 quart chicken stock
1 medium head of cabbage, shredded
6 small red potatoes, cubed

2 large Vidalia or sweet onions, chopped
1/2 cup Johnny Harris Bar-B-Cue Sauce, or
    BBQ Sauce, see recipe, p. 136
2 celery ribs, chopped
Salt and pepper to taste

In a large Dutch oven, cook the beef over medium heat for 8 to 10 minutes, or until it is no longer pink. Drain the meat in a colander, return it to the Dutch oven, and add the tomatoes, chicken stock, cabbage, potatoes, onions, barbecue sauce, and celery. Increase the heat to high and bring the soup to a boil, then reduce the heat to medium-low and simmer uncovered for 35 minutes, or until the vegetables are tender. Season with salt and pepper.

Shrimp Bisque

serves 6

2 (14.5-ounce) cans diced tomatoes, drained
2 1/2 cups beef broth
1 cup chopped celery
2 medium carrots, shredded
2 teaspoons chopped fresh parsley
4 whole cloves garlic, peeled
6 black peppercorns
1 bay leaf

2 teaspoons salt
3 tablespoons uncooked white rice
Pinch dried thyme
1 1/2 pounds medium shrimp, cooked, peeled,
    and deveined,
2 cups half-and-half
1/4 cup good quality sherry

Combine the tomatoes with the next 10 ingredients in a large saucepan over medium heat and simmer for 1 hour. Remove and discard the bay leaf. In a blender or food processor, puree the soup in batches until smooth, being careful to vent to allow steam to escape. Return the soup to the saucepan.

  Cut the cooked shrimp into 1/2-inch pieces and add to the soup along with the half-and-half. Over medium low heat, simmer until thoroughly heated. Ladle into individual bowls and sprinkle 2 teaspoons sherry on top of each serving.

Doug Matsuoka
manager since 1977

I answered an ad in 1977 for a job in Valdosta, Georgia, at a Dutch Pantry next to a Ramada Inn. I drove up from my home in Tallahassee to meet Mr. Donaldson. He didn't have a fancy office—papers were all piled up all over his desk—and I thought, "What am I getting into?" He was looking for a manager for another place over in Savannah—Johnny Harris's—so I went to see the restaurant and was immediately impressed by the age of the business and the beauty of the main dining room.

Johnny Harris Restaurant was a lot different then. The parking lot was unpaved and there was nothing but open fields on one side. The road wasn't too impressive at that time either, but the restaurant was hopping even though there was a recession going on, so I took the job.

I had the privilege of working with four of the older black waiters until they retired. Richard Worlds was one of these, and the guests loved him so much that they gave him a retirement party. He was close to 80 years old when he retired. He was always dignified, a real gentleman who took pride in his work.

I have met celebrities who came here to eat: Clint Eastwood, Robert Duvall, Senator Barry Goldwater, and Emma Kelly, the piano player who Johnny Mercer named "The Lady of 6,000 Songs." Of course, these are only a few of the celebrities who have dined with us.

Hearty Mushroom Soup

serves 8

½ cup pearl barley
2 medium carrots, finely chopped
1 medium Vidalia or sweet onion, chopped
2 cloves garlic, minced
¼ cup butter
2 pounds fresh button mushrooms, rinsed
   and chopped
4 cups beef broth

2 tablespoons all-purpose flour
2 cups heavy whipping cream
2 tablespoons Marsala wine
½ teaspoon salt
½ teaspoon pepper
Shaved Parmesan, for garnish
Fresh parsley, for garnish

Place the barley and carrots, along with 2 cups water, in a small saucepan over medium-high heat and bring to a boil. Reduce the heat and simmer for 20 to 25 minutes, or until most of the water is absorbed by the barley. Remove from the heat and set the cooked barley and carrots aside.

In a large saucepan over medium-low heat, sauté the onion and garlic in butter until tender. Reduce the heat to low, add the mushrooms, and cook 8 to 10 minutes more, stirring occasionally, until the mushrooms are tender.

In a small bowl, mix ½ cup beef broth with the flour, stirring to remove all the lumps. Add this flour mixture along with the cream, remaining broth, the Marsala wine, the cooked carrots, and barley to the mushrooms. Add the salt and pepper and continue to cook over low heat, stirring, until all ingredients are heated thoroughly and well-blended. You may want to add more beef broth if the liquid becomes too thick.

Ladle the soup into bowls and garnish with Parmesan cheese and fresh parsley.

Salads

Sweet Pea Potato Salad

serves 8 to 10

2 pounds red new potatoes, cut into 1-inch
   pieces
1 teaspoon salt
2 tablespoons cider vinegar
1 (10-ounce) package frozen peas
¾ cup mayonnaise

¾ cup sour cream
¼ cup chopped green onion
1 tablespoon dill weed
Freshly ground pepper to taste

Place the potatoes in a Dutch oven and add enough water to just cover. Bring the pot to a boil over high heat and add the salt. Turn the heat to low and simmer until the potatoes are tender. Use a slotted spoon to transfer the potatoes to a large bowl, sprinkle with salt and cider vinegar, and set aside.

Boil the peas according to package instructions in the same pot for 4 to 5 minutes, or until just tender. Drain and rinse the peas, then add them to the potatoes.

Whisk the mayonnaise and sour cream together in a small bowl, and stir in the green onions and dill weed. Add the sour cream mixture to the bowl of potatoes and peas and toss gently until well incorporated. Season with additional salt and pepper to taste. This salad may be served warm or chilled.

 **RECOLLECTIONS**

I grew up in Victory Manor in Savannah, just across the street from Johnny Harris Restaurant. My father, a local attorney, always took us there to dine, and fried chicken was my favorite as a young man. Around 1946 or 1947, when I was 4 or 5 years old, I ran away from home. I can't remember why. Where did I go? I went to Johnny Harris's, of course. When I walked in, the waiters recognized me and called my father to tell him where I was. While I waited for him to come from his downtown office to get me, I was treated to my favorite meal: fried chicken with barbecue sauce. It's still a favorite to this day. —Jim Glass

Layered Broccoli Salad

serves 8 to 10

6 cups chopped broccoli florets
1 small red onion, thinly sliced
2/3 cup dried sweetened cranberries, or raisins
1/2 cup plain yogurt
3 tablespoons honey
2 tablespoons mayonnaise

2 tablespoons cider vinegar
1 1/2 cups grated cheddar cheese
1/4 cup chopped walnuts, or sunflower seeds
2 pieces crisp bacon, crumbled

In a large glass serving bowl, arrange layers of broccoli, onion, and cranberries.
   In a small mixing bowl, whisk together the yogurt, honey, mayonnaise, and vinegar. Drizzle the dressing over the salad and sprinkle the cheese evenly over the top. Cover and refrigerate until you are ready to serve. Sprinkle with sunflower seeds or walnuts, and crumbled bacon before serving.

Macaroni Salad

serves 8 to 10

4 cups uncooked macaroni
1/2 red bell pepper, diced
2 green onions, trimmed and diced
1/3 cup sweet and spicy pickle relish
1/2 cup chopped black olives
1 teaspoon hot pepper sauce

1/2 teaspoon salt
1/2 teaspoon pepper
1/2 cup mayonnaise
1/2 cup milk
1 tablespoon red wine vinegar

In a large saucepan over medium-high heat, boil the macaroni until tender. Turn off the heat and let the macaroni soak in the hot water for several minutes.
   Meanwhile, dice the red pepper and green onion and transfer to a small bowl. Add the pickle relish, chopped olives, hot pepper sauce, salt, and pepper and stir to combine.
   Drain the macaroni through a large colander and rinse with cold water. Transfer to a large bowl and add the pepper and onion mixture to the macaroni. Stir in the mayonnaise, milk, and vinegar and stir until well blended. Refrigerate at least 2 hours before serving to allow the flavors to meld.

Tomato Aspic

serves 8

You are taking a step back into time with this recipe for Tomato Aspic. It's a classic recipe that you rarely see anymore, but it was a beloved staple at many bridal showers and ladies' luncheons in the South.

3 envelopes unflavored gelatin
4 cups tomato juice, divided
3 tablespoons Johnny Harris Bar-B-Cue Sauce, or BBQ Sauce, see recipe, p. 136
1 tablespoon prepared horseradish
2 teaspoons Worcestershire sauce
1 teaspoon hot pepper sauce
½ teaspoon celery salt

¼ cup finely chopped green bell pepper
1 tablespoon plus 1 teaspoon grated Vidalia or sweet onion
⅓ cup finely chopped celery
½ cup mayonnaise
Bib lettuce leaves for serving

In a medium saucepan, sprinkle the gelatin over 1 cup tomato juice and let it stand for 1 minute. Cook over medium heat, stirring constantly for 3 to 5 minutes, or until the gelatin dissolves. Remove and transfer the gelatin to a large bowl. Stir in the remaining 3 cups tomato juice, the barbecue sauce, horseradish, Worcestershire sauce, hot pepper sauce, and celery salt. Refrigerate, covered, until the tomato mixture is the consistency of unbeaten egg whites.

Place the bell pepper, onion, and celery in a food processor and pulse 3 to 4 times, then gently fold the vegetables into the chilled tomato mixture until fully incorporated. Spoon the aspic into 8 lightly-oiled individual ½-cup molds. Cover and refrigerate for at least 3 hours until firm. Unmold each aspic onto a salad plate layered with a lettuce leaf, and top each with a teaspoon of mayonnaise.

Shrimp Salad

makes 4 sandwiches

1 pound (31 to 35 count) unpeeled
  medium shrimp
1/3 cup finely chopped celery
1/2 teaspoon salt
1/8 teaspoon white pepper

1/2 cup mayonnaise
Johnny Harris Seafood Seasoning to taste,
  or Seafood Seasoning, see recipe, p. 138

Fill a large saucepan with water and bring to a boil over high heat. Add the shrimp and cook 5 to 7 minutes, or until the shrimp turn pink. Drain and allow to cool enough to handle, then peel the shrimp, chop them into 1/2-inch pieces, and place in a medium bowl. Add the next 4 ingredients to the bowl and mix well. Sprinkle with seafood seasoning to taste and stir well. You may add more mayonnaise as needed for desired consistency. To make sandwiches, place a layer of lettuce on toasted bread and spread with shrimp salad. Cover with toasted bread and slice.

Johnny's Summer Salad

serves 12

1 head Romaine lettuce
1 pound fresh baby spinach leaves
1 cup toasted pecan pieces
1 (11-ounce) can Mandarin oranges, drained
2 green onions, sliced
1 (8-ounce) can sliced water chestnuts, drained

Red Wine Dressing
1/2 cup extra virgin olive oil
4 tablespoons sugar
4 tablespoons red wine vinegar
1/2 teaspoon salt
Pepper to taste

Combine all ingredients in a large salad bowl.
  To make the salad dressing: Whisk together all ingredients in a small bowl.
  Pour the dressing over the salad and toss well to coat.

Ladies' Lunch Chicken Salad

serves 12

1 cup mayonnaise
1 teaspoon paprika
1 teaspoon Lawry's Seasoned Salt
1½ cups dried cranberries
1 cup chopped celery

½ cup minced green bell pepper
2 green onions, chopped
½ cup chopped pecans
4 cups cooked boneless chicken, cubed,
Pepper to taste

In a medium bowl, mix together the mayonnaise, paprika, and seasoning salt. Then blend in the cranberries, celery, bell pepper, onion and pecans. Add the chopped chicken and mix well, making sure meat is well coated. Season with black pepper to taste and refrigerate at least 1 hour before serving.

Homemade Coleslaw

serves 12

1 cup mayonnaise
½ cup buttermilk
⅓ cup sugar
2 tablespoons Johnny Harris Carolina
    Bar-B-Cue Sauce, or Carolina Mustard-Style
    BBQ Sauce, see recipe, p. 136
1 tablespoon cider vinegar
1 tablespoon celery seeds
1 teaspoon salt
¼ teaspoon pepper

1 medium cabbage (about 1½ pounds),
    shredded
2 large carrots, grated
2 tablespoons Vidalia or sweet onion

Stir together the first 8 ingredients in a large bowl. Add the shredded cabbage, carrots, and onion, and toss gently to incorporate. Cover and refrigerate for 2 to 3 hours.
   Serve as an accompaniment to any barbecue dish, or atop pulled-pork sandwiches.

The new place of Johnny Harris, located on Victory Drive, had its opening Saturday night. The dining and dancing establishment is one of the finest in this section. The arrangement and appointmenas are attractive.

JOHNNY HARRIS OPENS FINE PLACE

ATTRACTIVE ENTERTAINMENT CENTER ON VICTORY DRIVE

Johnny Harris opened his new handsome brick night club on Victory Drive Saturday and catered to large crowds there Saturday night and yesterday.

Equipped with the most modern furnishings; a polycon dance floor of 3,000 square feet, compared to 900 feet at the old place at Victory Drive and Bee road; air-cooled throughout; twenty-four booths opening on the dance floor; special rooms for parties, including the red room, blue room, and green room, and beautiful decorations, the new place affords Savannahians one of the most modern night clubs.

Music is furnished by an electric phonograph, the tones being equally distributed throughout the dance floor by loud speakers.

One of the attractive features of the dance floor is a miniature light house in the center of the floor with revolving decorative lights. The cool air escapes from this, diffusing throughout the place. Walls are of knotted cypress. Chairs are of chromium with leather upholstery and tables are of chromium with cafalite tops. The "powder puff room" is a special feature for the women patrons.

The bar, one of the most modern and attractive, is in a large room separate from the dance floor and booths. The kitchens, pantries, and ice boxes, or ice rooms, are equipped with the latest and best equipment and from these will be served Harris' famous barbecue, chicken and other dishes.

Larry Stack, formerly a steward with the Ocean Steamship Co., manager of the dining room. Kermit (Red) Donaldson is in charge of the kitchen and Robert Wallace is manager of the Maple room. John Moore and Tom Zupler, both well known to Harris patrons are on the staff.

Jeweled Fruit Salad

serves 12

1 pint fresh strawberries, sliced
1 ½ cups green seedless grapes, halved
1 (11-ounce) can Mandarin oranges, drained
1 cup fresh or frozen blueberries
1 cup fresh or frozen raspberries
1 medium kiwi fruit, peeled and chopped
¼ cup fresh or frozen cranberries, thawed
   and halved

Yogurt Dressing
1 (8-ounce) cup vanilla yogurt
2 tablespoons orange juice
1 tablespoon mayonnaise

Mix together all the fruit in a large serving bowl.

Whisk together the yogurt, orange juice, and mayonnaise in a separate bowl.

Using a ladle or large serving spoon, place ½ cup fruit into individual fruit cups and top with the yogurt dressing.

 **RECOLLECTIONS**

My father passed away when I was a child, and my mother returned to her native Savannah to raise four daughters. Mom made sure we were afforded one special treat every Friday night. We would all dress up, pile into the car, and go to Johnny Harris's for dinner. We felt like princesses in the big dining room with the twinkling stars on the ceiling and a little button at the end of the table to signal our waiter. My most heartwarming memory is of our favorite waiter, Walter Dozier. A large, dignified black man, Walter dressed in a black suit, white shirt, and black bow tie. He would ask my mom how her week had been and tell her that he had her drink, a Manhattan, waiting. Then he would insist that the "four little ladies" had their own Shirley Temple cocktails with extra cherries that he always made sure were included.

The memories of my time there will never fade, and new memories are made by us now for future generations of our family. —Marian Meyer Nelson

Joann Polite
Kitchen Supervisor

As kitchen supervisor, I take care of every order that comes in. I bring in our food stock and do the ordering and some of the cooking. I cook the specials, like chicken and turkey pot pie, chicken and dumplings, spaghetti, meatloaf, crab au gratin, and seafood au gratin. Plus I do all the cooking for catering jobs, except for the barbecue meats. I bake the yeast rolls and the coconut pie, too.

I've worked here 31 years. I started on the barbecue pit and worked my way to the kitchen. Today I have a staff of 17, which includes both the day and night shift.

My first job at Johnny Harris was on the pit. Miss Liza was the lady pitmaster at that time, and she showed me how to cook the meat and set it all up the Johnny Harris way. We had others who helped us on the pit, but at that time there were no pit men. Now we have Jason to make the barbecue, but back then the pit was run by women.

We would come in very early to barbecue the meat, wearing any old thing. Around 11:30 a.m., we would change into a white coat and a chef's hat and tie a scarf around our neck. We called it "showtime." Mr. Donaldson would come in the side door, raise his arms and say, "Get ready, it's showtime!"

Cranberry Walnut Spinach Salad

serves 8

⅔ cup olive oil
6 tablespoons sugar
4 tablespoons white wine vinegar
4 tablespoons sour cream
1 teaspoon ground mustard
1 (12-ounce) package baby spinach leaves
1 cup chopped walnuts
1 cup dried cranberries

Combine the olive oil, sugar, vinegar, sour cream, and mustard in a jar with a tight fitting lid and shake well.

Divide the spinach among 8 salad plates and drizzle with the dressing. Sprinkle each serving with the walnuts and cranberries.

Dilled Pea Salad

serves 6

1 (16-ounce) package frozen baby peas
¼ cup mayonnaise
¼ cup sour cream
1½ tablespoons horseradish
1½ tablespoons Dijon mustard
2 teaspoons dried dill weed
⅛ teaspoon fresh ground pepper
Red cabbage leaves, to plate
Dill sprigs, optional, for garnish

Cook the peas according to the package instructions, then drain and allow to cool.

Stir together the mayonnaise, sour cream, horseradish, Dijon mustard, dill weed, and pepper. Pour the mayonnaise mixture over the peas and stir gently to mix. Cover and refrigerate for at least 2 hours. When you are ready to serve, place a red cabbage leaf on each salad plate. Spoon the salad onto each leaf and garnish with a sprig of dill weed.

Cranberry and Wild Rice Salad

serves 8 to 10

4 cups white rice, cooked
4 cups wild rice, cooked
1 cup pecans, chopped, and toasted
1 cup dried cranberries, soaked in water for
    10 minutes and drained
1 cup green onions, minced
½ cup finely chopped celery
1 red bell pepper, chopped
⅓ cup parsley, minced

Vinaigrette Dressing
4 tablespoons rice vinegar
4 tablespoons lemon juice
1 clove garlic, minced
⅓ cup extra virgin olive oil
2 tablespoons sesame seed oil

Combine all the salad ingredients in a large bowl. Cover and refrigerate until ready to serve.
   Combine the vinaigrette dressing ingredients in a food processor and process until smooth. Toss the chilled salad with the vinaigrette dressing and serve.

Pear Lime Gelatin Salad

serves 8

1 (15-ounce) can pear halves
1 (3-ounce) package lime gelatin
1 (8-ounce) package cream cheese, cubed
1 can (20-ounce) unsweetened, crushed
    pineapple, drained

1 cup pecans, toasted and divided
1 (8-ounce) carton frozen whipped topping

Drain the pears, and reserve the juice in a small saucepan. Set the pears aside. Bring the reserved juice in the saucepan to a boil over medium-high heat. Add the gelatin, and stir until it dissolves. Remove the pan from the heat and allow to cool slightly.
   In a food processor, combine the pears and cream cheese, cover, and process until smooth. Transfer to a large bowl and stir in the gelatin mixture until well blended. Stir in the pineapple and ¾ cup of the pecans. Fold in the whipped topping, pour into an ungreased 11 x 7-inch dish, and refrigerate until set.
   Sprinkle with the remaining pecans and cut into squares to serve.

Orzo Salad with Broccoli and Onions

serves 6

1 pound orzo pasta
¼ extra virgin olive oil
1 (10-ounce) bag (2 cups) frozen pearl onions
Salt and freshly ground pepper
3 cloves garlic, minced
1 pound broccoli, cut into small florets
1 (15-ounce) can cannelloni beans, rinsed
  and drained
½ cup freshly grated Parmesan cheese

Dressing
Juice of 3 large lemons
¾ cup extra virgin olive oil
3 tablespoons honey
3½ teaspoons salt, divided
1¼ teaspoons freshly ground black pepper,
  divided
1 cup chopped chives

Bring a large pot of salted water to a boil over high heat, add the pasta and cook 8 to 10 minutes, or until tender. Drain and place the pasta in a large serving bowl.

In a medium saucepan, heat the oil over medium-high heat. Add the onions, season with a pinch of salt and pepper, and cook, stirring occasionally, for 5 to 7 minutes, until the onions are slightly golden and tender. Add the garlic and cook for 30 seconds more, then add the broccoli and sauté for an additional 1 minute. Add ⅓ cup water and use a wooden spoon to scrape up the brown bits that cling to the bottom of the pan. Cover the pan and cook for another 4 to 5 minutes, until the broccoli is tender. Add the beans and cook for 1 minute until just warmed through.

Transfer the broccoli and onion mixture to a serving bowl, add the Parmesan cheese, and toss with the orzo.

To make the dressing: In a small bowl, whisk together the lemon juice, olive oil, honey, ½ teaspoon salt, and ¼ teaspoon pepper. Stir in the chives. Pour the dressing over the salad, toss, and season with the remaining salt and pepper before serving.

Crunchy Corn Salad

serves 10

1 (12-ounce) bag (2 cups) frozen small
  green peas, thawed
1 (15.25-ounce) can whole kernel yellow
  corn, drained
1 (15.25-ounce) can shoepeg (white) corn,
  drained
1 (8-ounce) can water chestnuts, drained
  and chopped
1 jar diced pimentos, drained and chopped
8 green onions, thinly sliced
2 celery ribs, chopped
1 medium green pepper, finely chopped

Dressing
½ cup vinegar
½ cup sugar
¼ cup extra virgin olive oil
1 teaspoon salt
¼ teaspoon black pepper

In a large bowl, combine all the salad ingredients.

In a separate small bowl, combine all the dressing ingredients and whisk until the sugar is dissolved. Pour the dressing mixture over the corn mixture and mix well. Cover and refrigerate for at least 3 hours before serving. Stir again just before serving.

Red Pepper and Tomato Couscous Salad

serves 6

2 large red bell peppers
3 cups water
1½ cups pearled couscous, uncooked
1 small unpeeled cucumber, chopped
½ Vidalia or sweet onion, chopped
½ cup chopped fresh basil
¼ cup chopped fresh parsley
1 large ripe tomato, chopped

Dressing
3 tablespoons olive oil
¼ cup lemon juice, freshly squeezed
½ teaspoon salt
⅛ teaspoon pepper
½ teaspoon Dijon mustard

Roast the red peppers in a 350 degree F oven until the peppers are charred on all sides. Place the peppers in a zip-top bag, seal tightly, and place in the freezer for 15 minutes until the peppers are completely cool. Peel and seed the peppers and chop into ½-inch pieces.

Bring 3 cups water to boil in a medium saucepan over high heat and stir in the couscous. When the couscous has cooked according to package directions, remove from the heat and let the pot stand, covered, for 5 to 10 minutes or until all the water is absorbed.

To make the dressing, combine all the ingredients in a jar with a tight-fitting lid and shake until blended.

Combine the red peppers, couscous, cucumber, onion, basil, parsley, and tomato in a serving bowl. Mix well and toss with the dressing. Cover and refrigerate for 1 to 2 hours prior to serving.

Warm Red Potato Salad

serves 8 to 10

4 pounds small red new potatoes, quartered
10 bacon strips, chopped
1 large Vidalia or sweet onion, chopped
3 tablespoons chopped celery
2 tablespoons chopped green bell pepper
1 tablespoon all-purpose flour
1 tablespoon sugar
1 teaspoon salt
1/2 teaspoon pepper
1/3 cup white balsamic vinegar

Place the potatoes in a large Dutch oven with enough water to cover. Bring to a boil, then reduce the heat, cover, and simmer for 15 to 20 minutes, or until tender. Drain and place in a large serving bowl.

Meanwhile, cook the bacon in a large skillet over medium-high heat until crisp. Using a slotted spoon, transfer the bacon to paper towels to drain. Reserve the pan drippings.

To make the dressing: In the remaining bacon drippings, sauté the onion, celery, and bell pepper for 5 to 7 minutes over medium heat, or until tender. Stir in the flour, sugar, salt, and pepper until well blended.

Combine 1 cup water and the vinegar in a small bowl or cup and stir this into the vegetable mixture in the skillet. Bring the mixture to a boil and cook, stirring constantly, for 2 minutes, or until the dressing thickens.

Pour the dressing over the potatoes and toss well with the bacon bits. Serve warm or at room temperature.

Vegetables and Breads

Harris's Mac and Cheese

serves 6 to 8

3 cups uncooked macaroni
1 (8-ounce) package cream cheese, softened,
 and cut into 1-inch cubes
4 cups grated marbled cheddar cheese
3 tablespoons butter
3 large eggs
¾ cups half-and-half
Salt and pepper to taste

Preheat the oven to 350 degrees F.

In a large pot of boiling water, cook the macaroni according to package instructions. When the pasta is al dente, let it sit in the hot water to absorb for 10 minutes, then drain.

Put the cream cheese cubes in a large bowl and pour the hot macaroni on top. Let sit for 5 minutes to melt the cheese. Add 2 cups of the grated cheddar, the butter, eggs, half-and-half, salt, and pepper and stir until the cheeses are melted and the ingredients are well combined. Pour into a greased 9 x 13-inch baking dish. Top with the remaining shredded cheese and bake for 30 minutes, or until the cheese on top is melted and lightly browned.

 **RECOLLECTIONS**

When the restaurant was rebuilt in 1936 at the present site, the Grand Ballroom was designed with a lighthouse in the middle of the dance floor in the dining room, that revolved and had a light that shone out the top. We had to replace it because the revolving light made people dizzy if they were drinking and dancing.

The lighthouse structure became the housing for the first air-conditioning system in the city of Savannah. The cooled air was pumped in from an outdoor water tower and blown out through the structure in the middle of the room. It helped make the dancing more comfortable during the hot months. –Norman Hiedt

Okra and Tomatoes

serves 4 to 6

4 bacon slices
1 large sweet onion, chopped
1 garlic clove, minced
4 large tomatoes, cored and chopped
1 pound fresh okra, sliced into ½-inch pieces
1 (15-ounce) can tomato sauce

¼ cup Johnny Harris Bar-B-Cue sauce, or
 BBQ Sauce, see recipe, p. 136
Salt and pepper to taste
Hot cooked white rice

Cook the bacon in a large skillet or Dutch oven over medium heat until crisp. Drain on paper towels, then crumble the bacon.

Reserve 2 tablespoons bacon drippings in the skillet and sauté the onions and garlic over medium-high heat for 4 to 5 minutes, or until tender. Stir in the tomatoes, okra, tomato sauce, and barbecue sauce. Reduce the heat to medium-low and cook, stirring often, for 10 minutes or until the okra is tender. Salt and pepper to taste, serve over hot rice, and sprinkle with the reserved bacon crumbles.

Harris's Southern-Style Baked Beans

serves 12 to 18

8 slices bacon, chopped
1 medium sweet onion, diced
½ medium green bell pepper, diced
3 (28-ounce) cans baked beans,
 drained and rinsed
1 cup Johnny Harris Bar-B-Cue sauce, or
 BBQ Sauce, see recipe p. 136

¾ cup ketchup
¾ cup brown sugar
1 tablespoon cider vinegar
1 tablespoon Dijon mustard

Adjust oven rack to the lower middle position and preheat the oven to 300 degrees F.

In a skillet over medium-high heat, fry the bacon, drain on paper towels, and set aside.

Add the onions and peppers to the bacon drippings and sauté for 5 minutes, or until tender. Add the beans and all remaining ingredients and bring just to a simmer. Pour the beans into a greased 13 x 9-inch baking dish. Top with the bacon and bake 2 hours, until the beans are bubbly. Let stand at room temperature to allow the beans to thicken before serving.

BBQ Vidalias (Sweet Onions)

serves 8

8 large Vidalia or sweet onions, peeled and cored
8 tablespoons butter
1 teaspoon salt
1 teaspoon freshly ground pepper
1 cup Johnny Harris Bar-B-Cue Sauce, or
    BBQ Sauce, see recipe p. 136

Using a sharp knife, slice each onion into 4 wedges to within ½-inch of the root end. Place each onion on a 12-inch square of double-thick heavy-duty foil. Place 1 tablespoon butter in the center of each onion and sprinkle with salt and pepper. Coat each onion thoroughly with ⅛ cup of barbecue sauce. Fold the foil around the onions and seal tightly.

Prepare a grill for indirect heat. Grill the onions over medium heat for 35 to 40 minutes, or until tender. (They can also be baked in the oven at 350 degrees F for the same amount of time.) Open the foil carefully to allow steam to escape.

 **RECOLLECTIONS**

The restaurant had a zoo in back from 1937 to 1942 to occupy the children while their fathers played the slot machines and drank in the bar and back room. Many of the exotic birds, monkeys, and other animals were collected by Johnny Harris on several hunting expeditions.

In 1940, the Harrises took an orphaned monkey into their home as a pet. Mary Harris dressed it in baby clothes and pushed the monkey, which she named "Baby Girl," around town in a carriage. Consequently, the neighborhood children came to call Mary the "Monkey Lady." When Baby Girl grew too large to handle, she was donated to the Jacksonville Zoo and would reportedly greet the Harrises with squeals of joy whenever they visited her at the zoo. –Robert P. Harrod

Onion Rings

serves 8 to 10

2 extra-large Vidalia or sweet onions, peeled
    and sliced into ½-inch rings
1¾ cups all-purpose flour
½ cup self-rising cornmeal
1 tablespoon onion powder
1½ teaspoons salt

¾ teaspoon sugar
2 cups milk
1 egg, beaten
Vegetable oil

Separate all the onion rings and set aside.

To make the batter, combine the flour, cornmeal, onion powder, salt, sugar, milk, and egg in a large bowl and beat with a whisk until the lumps are gone.

In a large Dutch oven or heavy saucepan, add the oil to a depth of 2 to 3 inches, and heat to 375 degrees F.

Dip the onion rings in the batter to evenly coat, then fry in the hot oil for 1 minute on each side, or until they are golden brown on both sides.

Use long-handled tongs to remove and drain the cooked rings on paper towels. Serve immediately with ketchup or barbecue sauce.

RECOLLECTIONS

The Old Dixieland Drive-Through was next door to the restaurant. In the back was an old tree that became something to visit when you came to either Johnny Harris Tavern or the Old Dixieland Drive-Through. There was a guy who wanted to set the Guinness World Record for the number of days he could spend up in a tree; we called him the "tree-sitter," and everyone liked to go out back and check on him. –Launey Hiers III

Buttermilk Fried Okra

yields 8 cups / serves 6 to 8

1 pound fresh okra, cut into ¾-inch thick pieces
¾ cup buttermilk
1½ cups self-rising white cornmeal mix
1 teaspoon salt
1 teaspoon sugar
¼ teaspoon cayenne pepper
Vegetable oil, for frying

Stir together the okra and the buttermilk in a large bowl. Combine the cornmeal mix, salt, sugar, and cayenne in a separate large bowl. Remove the okra from the buttermilk in batches using a slotted spoon. Dredge the okra in the cornmeal mixture and then place in a colander. Shake off the excess cornmeal.

Pour oil to a depth of 1 inch in a large Dutch oven and heat to 375 degrees F. Fry the okra in batches about 4 minutes, or until golden brown, stirring gently to cook evenly. Remove the fried okra with a slotted spoon and drain on paper towels. Season with salt and pepper to taste.

Savannah Creamed Corn

serves 6 to 8

12 ears sweet corn, shucked and rinsed
½ cup (1 stick) butter
¾ teaspoon salt
1 teaspoon pepper
2 tablespoons sugar
2 tablespoons all-purpose flour
1 cup milk

With a sharp knife, remove the kernels of corn by slicing down the sides of the cobs. To get all the juices, hold the blade of the knife perpendicular to the cobs and scrape well, capturing the juices in a bowl. Place the corn kernels and juice, along with the butter, salt, pepper, and sugar in a heavy saucepan and cook over low heat for 15 minutes, stirring frequently to avoid scorching.

In a mixing bowl, add the flour to the milk and stir well to remove any lumps. Add the milk mixture to the saucepan with the corn and continue to simmer until the mixture thickens. Add additional milk if necessary to achieve desired consistency.

Carrot Soufflé

serves 8 to 10

2 pounds carrots, peeled and chopped
1/3 cup sugar
1/3 cup light brown sugar
1 1/2 teaspoons vanilla extract
1/2 cup butter

1 1/2 teaspoons baking powder
2 tablespoons all-purpose flour
1/2 teaspoon cinnamon
4 eggs, beaten
Powdered sugar, for dusting

Steam or boil the carrots until they are very tender. Drain well and transfer to a large mixing bowl or food processor. While the carrots are still warm, add the sugars, vanilla extract, and butter and process until smooth. This step may be done the day before and the carrot mixture refrigerated overnight.

Before baking, preheat the oven to 350 degrees F.

Allow the carrot mixture to come to room temperature.

Add the baking powder, flour, cinnamon, and beaten eggs to the carrot mixture and blend well. Pour the mixture into a 2-quart glass baking dish and bake for 1 hour, or until the top is lightly browned. Dust lightly with powdered sugar before serving.

Sweet Potato Soufflé

serves 6 to 8

4 cups (about 4 large), sweet potatoes,
   cooked, and mashed
1 cup sugar
3 eggs, lightly beaten
⅓ cup butter, softened
1 teaspoon vanilla
½ teaspoon salt

Topping
⅓ cup butter, softened
1 cup light brown sugar
1 cup shredded coconut
1 cup chopped pecans
⅓ cup self-rising flour

Preheat the oven to 300 degrees F.

In a large mixing bowl, combine the sweet potatoes, sugar, eggs, butter, vanilla, and salt and stir until well blended. Pour into a greased 2-quart baking dish.

To prepare the topping: Cream together the butter and brown sugar. Add the coconut, pecans, and flour and mix well. Spread over the top of the sweet potatoes.

Bake for 35 to 40 minutes, or until light golden brown.

 **RECOLLECTIONS**

I remember celebrating all our family "milestones" at Johnny Harris'. Richard Worlds was "our" waiter, and we always had booth #9. He could take orders for 20 and never write a thing down, and everyone's order would be perfect every time.

My parents would bribe me with Johnny Harris's cheese spread and coconut pie when they wanted me to stay home with a sitter while they were out carousing. On these nights, they always asked Richard to make me a "doggie bag" to go. When I was old enough to go there with them, or was invited —not on a dance night, of course—Richard would bring my pie without ever being asked. —Sonja Floyd Fishkind Springer

Black-Eyed Peas, Southern Style

serves 8

2 cups dried black-eyed peas, washed
2 slices salt pork
¾ cup sweet onion, minced
2 teaspoons salt

Place the peas in a large Dutch oven with 12 cups hot water, the salt pork, onion, and salt. Cover and bring to a boil, then reduce the heat and simmer for 2 to 3 hours, or until tender. Drain and serve hot. These peas are good served over white rice, too.

Hot Sherried Fruit

serves 6 to 8

1 fresh pineapple, cored and cut into
    1-inch chunks
4 large ripe peaches, peeled, pitted,
    and sliced
4 ripe pears, peeled and sliced
2 ripe apricots, peeled, pitted, and sliced
1 small jar maraschino cherries

1 ½ sticks butter
2 tablespoons cornstarch
¾ cup light brown sugar
1 teaspoon mild curry powder
1 cup dry sherry

Arrange the fruit in layers in a 2½-quart baking dish.

Cook the last 5 ingredients in a double boiler over medium heat, stirring constantly, until the sauce is thick and smooth. Pour the hot sauce over the fruit, cover the dish, and refrigerate overnight.

Before baking, remove the sherried fruit from the refrigerator and let it sit for 20 minutes. Bake uncovered at 325 degrees F for 45 minutes, or until hot and bubbly. Serve warm.

Asparagus and Green Onion Risotto

serves 6

2 tablespoons butter
¾ cup chopped green onions
½ teaspoon chopped fresh thyme
1½ cups uncooked Arborio rice (short grain)
5 cups chicken broth
½ pound fresh asparagus, cut into 1-inch lengths
⅓ cup freshly grated Parmesan cheese

Melt the butter in a large heavy saucepan over medium heat. Add the green onions and thyme and sauté for 1 to 3 minutes, or until the onions are soft. Add the rice, stirring to coat. Add 2½ cups chicken broth and bring to a boil, then reduce the heat to medium-low and simmer, stirring occasionally, for 15 minutes.

Add ½ cup chicken broth and cook until the liquid is absorbed, stirring constantly. Repeat this procedure with the remaining broth, adding ½ cup broth at a time. The total cooking time should be about 20 minutes.

Stir in the asparagus and simmer for 5 minutes, or until the asparagus is tender and the mixture is creamy. Stir in the Parmesan cheese and serve immediately.

Stewed Tomatoes and Onions

serves 6 to 8

4 tablespoons all-purpose flour
2 tablespoons brown sugar
4 tablespoons butter
5 cups peeled fresh tomatoes, coarsely chopped
2 Vidalia or sweet onions, sliced
Salt and pepper to taste

Combine the flour and sugar in a small bowl and set aside.

Melt the butter in a medium saucepan and add the tomatoes, onions, salt, and pepper. Stir in the flour/sugar mixture and cook on low heat for 30 minutes, stirring ocassionally, until the onions are soft.

Asparagus with Red Bell Pepper and Shallots

serves 8 to 10

2 pounds fresh asparagus, trimmed
1/3 cup unsalted butter
3 shallots, chopped
1 red bell pepper, julienned
1 clove garlic, minced
1 teaspoon salt
1/2 teaspoon freshly ground black pepper

After trimming any tough ends off the asparagus, blanch in boiling water over high heat for 3 to 4 minutes, or until the asparagus is just tender. Drain and set aside.

In a saucepan over medium-high heat, sauté the shallots, bell pepper strips, and garlic in the butter for 3 to 4 minutes, or until tender. Add the asparagus and toss with salt and pepper.

Fresh Cranberry Relish

yields 2½ cups

12 ounces fresh or frozen cranberries
1/3 cup sugar, or more as needed
1/3 cup orange juice
1/4 cup orange liqueur
3 tablespoons orange marmalade

If using fresh cranberries, wash and pick through them, then dry thoroughly.

In a medium saucepan, mix 1/3 cup of sugar, the cranberries, orange juice, orange liqueur, and the orange marmalade. Taste to adjust the sweetness and add more sugar if necessary. Simmer over medium-high heat, stirring occasionally, for about 10 minutes, until the berries are tender and have popped. Serve hot or cold, as a side dish with your holiday turkey.

Honey-Butter Grilled Corn

serves 6

2 tablespoons plus 1½ teaspoons butter
½ cup honey
2 large cloves garlic, minced
2 tablespoons hot pepper sauce
½ teaspoon salt

¼ teaspoon pepper
¼ teaspoon paprika
6 medium ears sweet corn, husked

Melt the butter in a small saucepan over medium heat and stir in the honey, garlic, pepper sauce, and seasonings just until blended and heated through. Brush this honey-butter over the corn when you are ready to grill.

Moisten a paper towel with cooking oil and, using long-handled tongs, lightly coat a grill rack. Heat the grill to medium-high.

Wrap each cob separately in aluminum foil and place them on the grill to cook for 15 to 20 minutes, turning a quarter-turn every 3 to 5 minutes. When done, unwrap the cobs and serve hot.

Spinach with Artichoke Hearts

serves 6 to 8

1 (8-ounce) package cream cheese, softened
½ cup (1 stick) butter, softened
Juice of 1 lemon
2 (10-ounce) packages chopped frozen
 spinach, cooked
1 (14-ounce) can artichoke hearts, drained
 and sliced

Preheat the oven to 350 degrees F.

In a medium bowl, mix the cream cheese, butter, and lemon juice. Drain the spinach and stir into the cream cheese mixture.

Place the sliced artichoke hearts in the bottom of a greased casserole dish and top with the spinach mixture. Bake for 15 minutes, until heated thoroughly.

Yellow Squash Casserole

serves 6

6 to 8 yellow squash, sliced
1 medium onion, chopped
¾ cup sour cream
2 eggs, beaten
1½ cups grated sharp cheddar cheese

Preheat the oven to 350 degrees F.

Place the squash and onions in a saucepan, cover with water, and bring to a boil over high heat. Cook until the squash and onions have softened, then drain and mash in a large bowl. Add the sour cream, eggs, and ¾ cup cheese and stir to combine. Pour the squash mixture into a 2-quart baking dish. Top with the remaining cheese and bake for 1 hour, until the casserole is bubbly and the edges are lightly browned.

Green Beans with Pecan Brown Butter

serves 4 to 6

3 pounds thin green beans (haricot verts-style)
6 tablespoons unsalted butter
1 cup pecans, chopped
2 cloves garlic, minced
1 teaspoon salt
½ teaspoon freshly ground black pepper
¼ cup finely chopped flat-leaf parsley

Cook the beans in boiling salted water for 4 to 5 minutes, or until they are crisp/tender. Transfer to a bowl of ice cold water to halt the cooking, and drain well.

Melt the butter in a large heavy skillet over medium heat and cook for 3 minutes, stirring occasionally, until lightly browned and fragrant. Stir in the pecans and garlic and cook 2 minutes more. Add the green beans, salt, and pepper, and cook for 4 minutes, stirring, until heated through. Sprinkle with fresh parsley before serving.

Spicy BBQ Deviled Eggs

yields 2 dozen

12 eggs
½ cup mayonnaise
¼ cup Johnny Harris Carolina Mustard
   Bar-B-Cue Sauce, or Carolina Mustard-Style
   BBQ Sauce, see recipe, p. 136

1 teaspoon Dijon mustard
½ to 1 teaspoon hot pepper sauce
¼ teaspoon salt
2 teaspoons finely chopped parsley

Place the eggs in a large Dutch oven and cover with enough cool water to cover by 1 or 2 inches. Slowly bring the eggs to a boil over medium-high heat, and boil gently for 1 minute, then turn off the heat and cover the pot. Let the eggs sit in the hot water for 15 to 20 minutes, then place the pot under a faucet and slowly add cool water to displace the hot water. Lift the eggs out using a slotted spoon and place them on a towel to dry. Peel the eggs, then slice each in half lengthwise. Scoop out the yolks and place them in a medium bowl. Arrange the egg white halves on a serving platter.

Mash the yolks with a fork and add the mayonnaise, barbecue sauce, mustard, hot pepper sauce, and salt. Stir the egg mixture until smooth and creamy, and season with more salt and pepper if desired. Spoon or pipe the egg mixture into the egg white halves, and sprinkle with chopped parsley. Serve immediately or refrigerate until ready to serve.

 **RECOLLECTIONS**

The origin of Johnny Harris's Bar-B-Cue Sauce was a bit of a mystery. Johnny Harris, along with an elderly black barbecue cook from Virginia, John Moore, created the original "Bar-B-Cue Sauce" recipe in 1925, which was an immediate hit with customers. The first recipe was not written down but was relegated to the memory of Moore and Harris. Later, Johnny wrote the recipe down and shared it with his closest business associates and family members. This recipe is now in a safety deposit box.

The recipe for Johnny Harris Bar-B-Cue Sauce calls for cooking ingredients without using thickeners. Many barbecue sauces are just mixed ingredients. Later the family had the sauce kosher certified for their many Jewish customers.

Buttermilk Garlic Mashed Potatoes

serves 6 to 8

3 pounds russet potatoes, peeled and cubed
2 tablespoons butter
3 garlic cloves, chopped
2 cups buttermilk

⅔ cup milk
½ teaspoon salt
½ teaspoon pepper

Fill a large Dutch oven with cold water. Add the potatoes and enough water to cover them, bring to a boil, then reduce the heat and simmer for 20 minutes until tender. Drain the water and set the potatoes aside in a bowl.

Melt the butter in the same Dutch oven over medium heat, then sauté the garlic for 1 minute. Stir in the buttermilk, milk, salt, and pepper and continue to cook for 5 minutes, stirring constantly, until thoroughly heated. Add the cooked potatoes and mash with a potato masher until they are smooth. Use more milk if needed to achieve desired consistency.

Twice-Baked Sweet Potatoes

serves 8

8 large sweet potatoes
Vegetable oil
1½ cups chopped pecans, divided
1 cup golden raisins

½ cup firmly packed brown sugar
½ cup (1 stick) butter, softened
½ teaspoon salt
1 cup miniature marshmallows

Preheat the oven to 350 degrees F.

Line a baking sheet with foil. Rub the skins of the potatoes with oil to coat, place them on the prepared baking sheet, and bake for 1 hour, until tender. Let them cool enough to handle, then cut a thin slice off the top of each potato lengthwise, being careful not to damage the skins. Scoop out the pulp with a spoon, leaving the shells ⅛-inch thick.

In a medium mixing bowl, combine the sweet potato pulp, 1 cup pecans, the raisins, brown sugar, butter, and salt. Stir well to combine. Spoon the mixture into the sweet potato shells and return the filled potatoes to the prepared baking sheet. Top with marshmallows and sprinkle with the remaining ½ cup pecans. Bake 20 to 25 minutes and serve immediately.

Pinto Beans with Smoked Ham Hock

serves 6

4 cups dried pinto beans, sorted and rinsed
3 ½ teaspoons salt, divided
2 cups chicken broth
1 ½ cups Vidalia or sweet onions, chopped
½ cup red bell pepper, finely chopped
¼ teaspoon crushed red pepper
1 smoked ham hock
2 cloves garlic, minced
2 tablespoons Johnny Harris Steak Sauce, or
   Steak Sauce, see recipe, p. 137, or
   substitute 1 teaspoon Worcestershire sauce

In a large Dutch oven over high heat, add the beans, 2 teaspoons salt and enough water to cover the beans by 2 inches. Bring to a boil, then cover and remove the pot from the heat. Let the beans stand, covered, for 1 hour, then drain in a colander and return the beans to the pot.

   Add 2 cups water, the remaining salt, and the chicken broth, chopped onions, bell pepper, crushed red pepper, ham hock, and minced garlic to the beans. Cover and bring the pot to a boil, then reduce the heat and simmer, partially covered, for 2 to 2½ hours, or until the beans are very tender. Additional water may be added if needed. Serve with Sweet Country Cornbread (see recipe, p. 125).

Roasted Brussels Sprouts with Walnuts

serves 6 to 8

3 pounds medium Brussels sprouts
4 tablespoons olive oil
2 tablespoons balsamic vinegar
1 teaspoon freshly ground black pepper
¾ cup chopped walnuts
Salt to taste

Preheat the oven to 375 degrees F.

Wash the sprouts and trim the bottoms. Cut the Brussels sprouts in half, lengthwise. Place the sprouts in a large saucepan with enough water to cover and boil over high heat for about 5 minutes. Drain and add the olive oil, vinegar, and black pepper to the saucepan and stir well to coat.

Cover a sheet pan with foil and spray with cooking spray. Spread the sprouts out on the pan and bake for 10 minutes. Stir to redistribute and bake for another 10 minutes. Sprinkle with the walnuts and bake for an additional 5 minutes. Transfer to a serving dish, salt to taste, and serve immediately.

Garlic Cheddar Grits

serves 6 to 8

1 (32-ounce) carton chicken broth
1 cup stone ground white grits, uncooked
1 cup half-and-half
3 large cloves garlic, minced

1 teaspoon salt
1½ cups shredded sharp cheddar cheese
3 tablespoons butter
¼ teaspoon ground white pepper

In a medium saucepan, heat the chicken broth and 1 cup water over medium-high heat. Add the grits and stir well. Bring to a boil, then reduce the heat and simmer, stirring frequently, for 1 hour.

Stir in the half-and-half, garlic, and salt and simmer for another 45 minutes, stirring frequently, until the grits thicken. Remove from the heat and stir in the cheese, butter, and white pepper until the cheese has melted. Serve hot.

Vidalia Onion Rolls

yields 16 rolls

3 tablespoons olive oil
1 large Vidalia onion, diced
¼ cup plus 1 teaspoon sugar
1 teaspoon salt
2 (.25-ounce) packages dry yeast

2 large eggs
6 tablespoons unsalted butter, melted
6 cups all-purpose flour

Heat 2 tablespoons olive oil in a large skillet over medium-high heat. Add the onions, 1 teaspoon sugar, and ½ teaspoon salt and cook, stirring occasionally, for 15 minutes, or until the onions begin to brown.

Place 2 cups warm tap water in a large bowl and sprinkle with the yeast. Let stand 4 to 5 minutes, until it begins to foam. Whisk in the eggs, 4 tablespoons butter, the remaining ¼ cup sugar, and ½ teaspoon salt. Add the flour and ¾ of the onion and mix until the dough becomes sticky. Transfer the dough to a large bowl and brush the top with the remaining 1 tablespoon oil.

Cover the bowl with plastic wrap and let the dough rise 1 hour in a warm place until it doubles in bulk.

Butter a 9 x 13-inch baking pan.

Punch the dough down. With well-floured hands, form the dough into 16 balls and place in the prepared pan, spacing evenly. Sprinkle the rolls with the remaining onions. Cover the pan loosely with plastic wrap and let the dough rise in a warm place another 30 to 40 minutes, until it has doubled again.

Heat the oven to 400 degrees F.

Remove the plastic wrap and brush the dough with the remaining 2 tablespoons butter. Bake the rolls for 18 to 22 minutes, or until the tops are golden. (Place a foil tent over the rolls if the tops seem to be browning too quickly.) Let the rolls cool in the pan for 5 minutes before serving.

Hush Puppies

yields 2 dozen

1 cup yellow cornmeal
¾ cup self-rising flour
¾ teaspoon garlic salt
½ teaspoon baking soda
½ cup finely chopped Vidalia or sweet onion

1 tablespoon chopped green onion
¾ cup buttermilk
1 large egg
Vegetable oil, for frying

In a medium bowl, combine the cornmeal, flour, garlic salt, and baking soda. Add the Vidalia onions and green onions and stir well.

In a small bowl, whisk the buttermilk and egg until smooth. Add this to the cornmeal mixture, and stir to combine.

In a Dutch oven, pour oil to a depth of 2 inches and heat to 325 degrees F. Drop the batter by tablespoonsful into the hot oil. Fry for 3 to 4 minutes, turning, until the hush puppies are golden brown on all sides. Remove with a slotted spoon and drain on paper towels. Serve warm.

Sweet Country Cornbread

serves 6 to 8

⅓ cup butter, softened
⅔ cup sugar
2 eggs
1½ cups all-purpose flour
1 cup yellow cornmeal
3 teaspoons baking powder

1 teaspoon salt
1 cup milk
1 cup sour cream
1 cup creamed corn
1 cup fresh or frozen sweet corn kernels

Preheat the oven to 375 degrees F.

In a large bowl, cream the butter, sugar, and eggs.

In another bowl, sift together the flour, cornmeal, baking powder, and salt. Add the flour mixture to the butter mixture and stir to combine. Add the milk, sour cream, creamed corn, and corn kernels and mix until all the ingredients are well incorporated. Pour the batter into a well-greased 9 x 9-inch baking dish and bake for 30 minutes, or until the top is light golden brown and a toothpick inserted in the center comes out clean.

Lemony Angel Biscuits

yields 2 dozen

2¼ teaspoons (1 packet) active dry yeast
2 cups milk
Juice and zest of 1 lemon
5 cups all-purpose flour
¼ cup sugar

1 teaspoon baking soda
1 teaspoon baking powder
1 teaspoon salt
1 stick cold unsalted butter, cubed

In a small bowl, stir the yeast into ½ cup tepid water. Continue to stir for 1 minute until the yeast is dissolved. Using a large measuring cup, combine the milk and lemon juice and set aside.

In a large bowl, whisk together the flour, sugar, baking soda, baking powder, and salt. Add the lemon zest and use your fingers to incorporate it into the other dry ingredients. Add the butter to the flour mixture using a pastry cutter, and blend until the dough is the consistency of large crumbs. Add the yeast mixture and the milk/lemon juice, stirring quickly to combine. Stir just until moistened, then cover and refrigerate for at least 2 hours.

Heat the oven to 450 degrees F.

Place the chilled dough on a lightly-floured work surface. Knead gently until the dough becomes easy to pat out into a circle about ¾-inch thick. Use a 2-inch biscuit cutter to form biscuits, gathering the scraps to use for extra biscuits.

Place the biscuits 1 inch apart on an ungreased baking sheet lined with foil and bake for 12 minutes, or until golden brown. Serve warm with jam or butter.

Yeast Rolls

yields 2 dozen rolls

½ cup sugar, plus a pinch
3 packages active dry yeast
2 teaspoons salt
3 eggs, well beaten

4½ cups all-purpose flour
⅓ cup solid shortening
2 tablespoons butter, melted

In a large mixing bowl, add a pinch of sugar to ½ cup warm water. Sprinkle the yeast over the water and let it stand undisturbed for 5 minutes, or until the water becomes foamy. Stir gently to fully dissolve the yeast.

Beat in the remaining sugar, the salt, eggs, and 1 cup cold water. With an electric blender on low speed, beat in 2 cups of flour for 2 minutes. Add the shortening and beat for 1 minute more. Add the remaining flour, ½ cup at a time, to make a soft dough ball. Place the dough in a well-greased bowl and turn to coat the dough. Cover with a towel and let rise 1 ½ hours, until the dough has doubled in bulk.

Punch the dough down and refrigerate, covered, overnight, or for 8 hours. The dough will almost double in bulk again. Place the dough on a floured surface and pull off pieces about ¼-cup in size to make 24 rolls.

Grease 2 (9-inch) round cake pans. Place 12 rolls in each pan, with the dough balls touching. Brush the tops with butter and place the pans in a warm place for 1 hour, or until the rolls have doubled in size.

Preheat the oven to 425 degrees F. Bake the rolls for 15 minutes, or until they are browned on top. Transfer the pans to a wire rack to cool slightly before serving.

Cheddar Biscuits

yields 2 dozen

3½ cups minus 1 teaspoon all-purpose flour
2 tablespoons baking powder
1 teaspoon salt
9 tablespoons plus 1 teaspoon cold unsalted
    butter
2 cups grated sharp cheddar cheese

1¾ cups buttermilk
1 large egg
3 tablespoons melted butter
1 teaspoon garlic salt
½ teaspoon parsley

Combine the flour, baking powder, and salt in a bowl and refrigerate for 20 to 30 minutes.

In the meantime, cut the butter into chunks and leave out at room temperature.

Position a rack in the center of the oven and heat to 400 degrees F.

Line 2 baking sheets with parchment paper.

Combine the chilled dry ingredients with the butter and cheese in the bowl of a standing mixer fitted with the paddle attachment, and mix on low speed until the chunks of butter are no bigger than a large pea. Add the buttermilk to the bowl and continue to mix on low until the dough just comes together. Turn the dough out onto a floured surface and gently knead a few times, using a dusting of flour if the dough is too moist.

Quickly and carefully pat the dough into a large rectangle about ½-inch thick. Using a 3-inch biscuit cutter, and cut the biscuits with a downward motion. Do not twist the cutter, as this will make the edges tough. Place the biscuits onto baking sheets, leaving about 1 inch between each one.

Beat the egg with a splash of water and gently brush the tops of the biscuits with the egg wash. Bake for 15 minutes, until lightly browned.

Meanwhile, mix the melted butter, garlic salt, and parsley together in a small bowl. After removing the biscuits from the oven, quickly brush the tops with the melted butter/garlic mixture. Bake 5 more minutes until the biscuits are deep golden brown, then cool slightly before serving.

Baking Powder Biscuits

yields 16 biscuits

2 cups all-purpose flour
1 tablespoon baking powder
2 teaspoons sugar

½ teaspoon salt
1⅓ cups whipping cream
2 tablespoons butter, melted

Preheat the oven to 425 degrees F.

Combine the flour, baking powder, sugar, and salt in a large bowl. Make a well in the center of the flour mixture, add the whipping cream all at once, and use a fork to stir until just moistened.

Place the dough in the center of a floured work surface and knead 12 times, repeatedly folding the dough over and pressing down. Gently pat the dough into an 8-inch square. Using a sharp knife or pastry cutter, slice the dough into 16 squares. Place the biscuits 1 inch apart on a large ungreased baking sheet and brush the top of each biscuit with melted butter. Bake for 12 minutes or until the tops are golden brown.

Jason Hampton

Pitmaster

I have been pitmaster at Johnny Harris Restaurant since 1999.

I work 9 to 3 on most days, and make all the barbecue pork, ribs, and lamb. We usually cook about 150 pounds of barbecue meat and serve it fresh daily. If I need to cater a party, I will cook even more. I sometimes work with an assistant—on holidays and for big parties—but most of the time it's just me on the pit.

I learned to barbecue from the former pitmaster here, and from watching guys on the streets of the city, pulling their big grills behind their cars to cookouts.

I love the adrenaline rush of cooking all this food, and I'm good at it. When you cook the same thing every day, how could you not become good at it?

Charlie Parlor

Nighttime Kitchen Supervisor

I have worked at Johnny Harris for 13 years—first as a dishwasher, then I moved on to salads, was a nighttime line cook, then was promoted to night supervisor.

I cook the steaks, crabcakes, stuffed flounder, and Marsala chicken. Older customers who know me will ask the waiters, "Is Charlie cooking the steaks tonight?" They like my steaks.

I learned to cook from my mother and grandmother; and Joann, the daytime kitchen supervisor, also taught me a lot. She was tough on me, making sure I did everything right, but she's a piece of my heart, that's for sure.

Now I have three or four people on the team I oversee, depending on the night. I like to stay busy, so this is a good job for me.

Sweet Potato Biscuits with Maple Butter

yields 18 biscuits

2 cups all-purpose flour
4 teaspoons baking powder
½ teaspoon salt
6 tablespoons cold butter, cut into cubes
1 large sweet potato, cooked and mashed
½ cup buttermilk, plus additional as needed

Maple Butter
1 stick unsalted butter, room temperature
3 tablespoons real maple syrup (not pancake syrup)

Preheat the oven to 375 degrees F.

In a large bowl, mix together the flour, baking powder, and salt. Using a pastry blender, cut the butter into the flour mixture until the dough resembles small peas.

In a separate bowl, whip the mashed sweet potato and buttermilk together until smooth. Fold this into the flour mixture until the dough forms a nice, slightly sticky ball. Add up to 4 tablespoons buttermilk as needed. Refrigerate the dough for 30 minutes and then place on a lightly-floured surface. Pat the dough out to a 1-inch thickness. Using a well-floured biscuit cutter, cut out rounds and place them on a large baking sheet about 1 inch apart. Gather up all the scraps and re-use to make extra biscuits.

Bake the biscuits for 15 minutes. Allow the biscuits to cool slightly, then top the warm biscuits with the maple butter.

To make the maple butter: Mix the butter and syrup together until a smooth consistency is achieved. Serve over the warm biscuits, or refrigerate until needed.

 **RECOLLECTIONS**

The original Bar-B-Cue sauce became so popular that customers would ask to take some home. We used to fill Coke bottles or liquor bottles with sauce and sell them that way. The grocery stores couldn't sell it because it was illegal to sell anything in a Coke bottle except Coke, but we sold them at the restaurant and out of the back of Red Donaldson's station wagon until the 1950s when the bottling plant was built. —Philip Donaldson

Sweet Potato and Carrot Spoon Bread

serves 10 to 12

1½ pounds sweet potatoes, peeled and
    cut into 1-inch pieces
1 pound carrots, peeled and cut into 1-inch
    pieces
2 cups milk
¼ cup yellow cornmeal
2 tablespoons butter, cubed
2 tablespoons ground cinnamon

½ teaspoon salt
½ cup all-purpose flour
½ cup pure maple syrup
½ cup whipping cream
4 egg yolks, lightly beaten
4 egg whites
Honey, to garnish

Preheat the oven to 400 degrees F.

Grease a 3-quart baking dish and set aside.

In a large pot over high heat, bring the potatoes and carrots to a boil in lightly salted water and cook for 20 to 25 minutes, or until tender. Drain and return the vegetables to the pot. Use a potato masher to mash the potatoes and carrots until nearly smooth. Set aside.

In a medium saucepan, combine the milk, cornmeal, butter, cinnamon, and salt. Bring the pan to boil over medium heat, stirring constantly, then reduce the heat and simmer, uncovered, for 5 minutes, or until the liquid slightly thickens. Remove the pan from the heat and allow to cool slightly.

In a large bowl, combine the mashed potato/carrot mixture, the cornmeal mixture, flour, maple syrup, whipping cream, and egg yolks.

In a medium bowl beat the egg whites with an electric mixer on medium-high speed until stiff peaks form.

Gently fold the beaten egg whites into the batter. Pour the batter into the prepared baking dish and bake 40 minutes, or until top is golden brown and the center feels firm to the touch. Drizzle servings with honey before serving, or pass the honey pot around the table. Serve warm.

Sauces, Rubs, and Meats

In 1924, the original Johnny Harris Restaurant used an open pit behind the tavern to barbecue meat. In the 1936 "new" building, an indoor pit was designed so that customers could see the meat cooking. The remnants of this pit and its tiled hood can still be seen in the Kitchen seating area. Our current gas barbecue "pit" is located in the back kitchen.

Oak wood or apple wood is soaked in water and loaded into the bottom of the current smoker. The wood flavor adds just a hint of smokiness to the meat.

Barbecue sauces are meant to enhance the flavor of barbecued meat. The Original Johnny Harris Bar-B-Cue Sauce marries the mustard flavor of the Carolinas to the tomato-based sauces of Georgia and Tennesse, creating a unique peppery sauce.

A few tips to remember when cooking with a barbecue sauce are: Never apply tomato-based sauce to meat early during cooking, as it may darken and burn. It should be used to baste the meat *after* it is thoroughly cooked. Baste ribs during the last 30 minutes of cooking, and baste chicken during the last 10 minutes of cooking. When grilling hamburgers, apply the sauce during the last 1 or 2 minutes on the grill. If you use sauces on other grilled meats, apply just before or after cooking is complete.

We hope you enjoy the sauce recipes included in this chapter. They reflect our most popular bottled sauces, including the original recipe; however, there is always a slight taste variation when creating a small consumer version versus a commercial sauce that is cooked in large quantities. Most people have a certain style of sauce they prefer with their barbecue, and we hope that, in using these recipes, you may be inspired to sample some of our many varieties of bottled sauces—or use these as a base to create your own personal version.

Many commercial sauce bottlers use a method in which they merely combine ingredients to become the sauce. Our sauces have always been cooked in a large kettle for at least 30 minutes to thoroughly marry all of the flavors and spices. Preparing a sauce recipe in a home kitchen can yield great results, and the following sauce recipes may be substituted in all recipes that call for the Johnny Harris Bar-B-Cue sauces.

BBQ Sauce

yields about 8 cups

⅓ cup dry mustard
3 cups vinegar
3½ cups ketchup
¼ cup plus 2 tablespoons sugar
4 tablespoons butter

⅛ cup hot pepper vinegar
2 teaspoons white pepper
1 teaspoon coarse black pepper
3 teaspoons salt
⅔ cup Worcestershire sauce

In a small bowl, beat together the mustard and 1 cup vinegar.

In a large Dutch oven or pot, add the vinegar mixture along with the rest of the ingredients. Whisk together over medium-high heat and continue to whisk for 15 minutes, until the sauce is an even consistency. Lower the heat to medium-low and simmer for 30 minutes, stirring occasionally. Pour into a sterilized, lidded container, and use immediately or refrigerate until ready to use.

Carolina Mustard-Style BBQ sauce

yields 2 cups

Sauces made from mustard are perfect to use with smoked barbecue pork. Mustard-based barbecue sauces have gained popularity as a signature sauce of South Carolina. They have their origins in the 18th century when German immigrants brought this style of sauce from Europe to the States and combined it with the indigenous pork barbecue.

1 cup prepared yellow mustard
½ cup cider vinegar
⅓ cup brown sugar
2 tablespoons butter
1 tablespoon hot pepper vinegar
1 tablespoon tomato paste

1 tablespoon Worcestershire sauce
1 tablespoon lemon juice
1 teaspoon white pepper
½ teaspoon salt
½ teaspoon black pepper

Mix all ingredients together in a saucepot and simmer over low heat for 30 minutes. Pour into a sterilized, lidded container and use immediately, or refrigerate until ready to use.

Steak Sauce

yields 2 cups

1 cup ketchup
½ cup Worcestershire sauce
¾ cup white vinegar
¼ cup lemon juice
2 tablespoons butter
2 tablespoons soy sauce
2 tablespoons prepared mustard
1 teaspoon brown sugar

1 teaspoon dry mustard
1 teaspoon white pepper
½ teaspoon onion powder
½ teaspoon garlic powder
Pinch ground cloves
6 drops liquid smoke

Combine all ingredients in a saucepan over medium heat and simmer, uncovered, for 30 minutes, stirring occasionally, until slightly thickened. Pour the sauce into a sterilized, lidded container and refrigerate until ready to use.

Spicy Honey BBQ Sauce

yields about 10 cups

3½ cups ketchup
3 cups vinegar
1½ cups light corn syrup
⅔ cup Worcestershire sauce
⅓ cup dry mustard
¼ cup plus 2 tablespoons sugar

4 tablespoons butter
3 teaspoons salt
⅛ cup hot pepper vinegar
2 teaspoon white pepper
1 teaspoon coarse black pepper
1 teaspoon cayenne

Mix all ingredients in a large, heavy saucepan over medium-high heat. Bring to a boil, then reduce the heat to simmer and cook for 30 minutes, stirring occasionally. Remove from the heat and let cool before transferring to a sterilized, lidded container. Use immediately or refrigerate until ready to use.

Seafood Seasoning

yields 1½ cups

4 bay leaves, finely ground
8 whole cloves, finely ground
1 cup celery salt
4 tablespoons sweet paprika
2 teaspoon black pepper
2 teaspoon cayenne
1 teaspoon dry mustard

1 teaspoon mace
½ teaspoon cinnamon
½ teaspoon allspice
½ teaspoon ginger

Grind the bay leaves and cloves using a coffee bean or spice grinder. Place all the ingredients in a tightly sealed zip-top bag and shake well to evenly mix. Store the sauce in a tightly sealed jar in a cool, dark, dry place. This seasoning will keep in a tightly-covered container for several months.

Honey Mustard Sauce

yields ½ cup

¼ cup mayonnaise
¼ cup Dijon mustard
2 tablespoons honey
1 tablespoon orange juice
Pinch garlic salt

Blend all ingredients in a small bowl or measuring cup. Use immediately or refrigerate until ready to use.

Horseradish Sauce

yields 1¼ cups

1 cup sour cream
¼ cup grated fresh horseradish
1 tablespoon Dijon mustard
1 teaspoon white wine vinegar
½ teaspoon garlic salt

Whisk all the ingredients together in a medium mixing bowl until the mixture is smooth and creamy. Cover the bowl with a lid or aluminum foil and refrigerate for at least 4 hours, or overnight to allow the flavors to meld. This sauce can be stored, tightly covered, in the refrigerator for up to 3 weeks.

BBQ Dry Rub

yields 2 cups

½ cup mild paprika
¼ cup kosher salt, finely ground
¼ cup brown sugar
¼ cup chili powder
¼ cup ground cumin
2 tablespoons mustard powder
1 tablespoon coarse black pepper
1 tablespoon white pepper
¼ cup granulated garlic
2 tablespoons cayenne

Combine all the ingredients in a medium bowl. Store in an air-tight container.

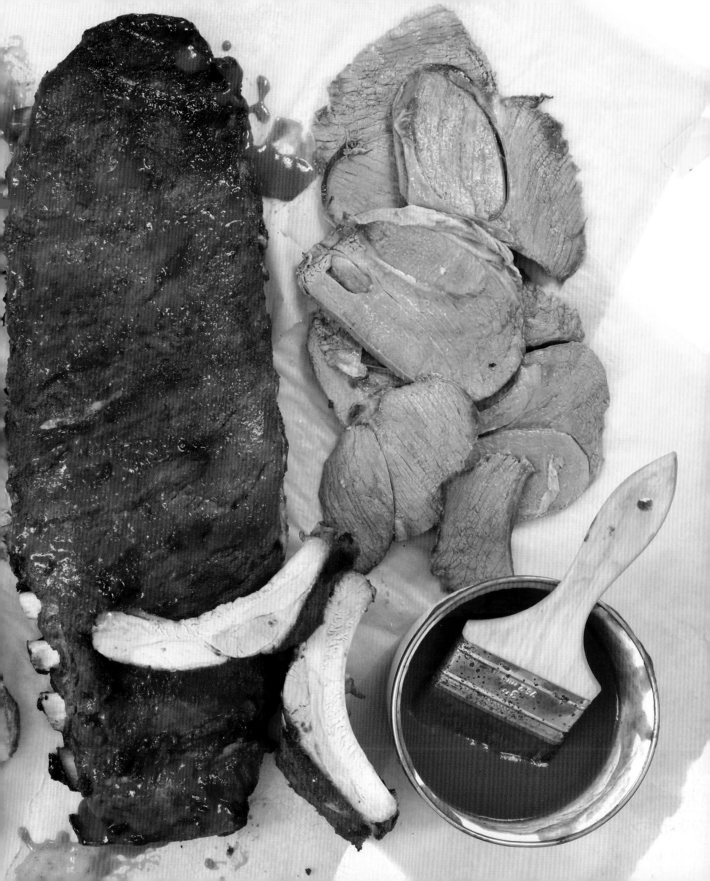

Slow-Cooked BBQ Pork

serves 12

1 (3 to 4-pound) shoulder pork roast
1 (12-ounce) can cola soft drink (not diet)
1 (18-ounce) bottle Johnny Harris Bar-B-Cue
  Sauce, or BBQ Sauce, see recipe, p. 136

Place the pork in a 6-quart slow cooker. Pour the entire can of cola over the roast, and then add the bottle of barbecue sauce. Cover tightly and cook on high heat for 6 to 7 hours until the meat is tender and shreds easily between two forks. Serve alone or on buns.

Bourbon and Peach Barbecue Chicken

serves 6 to 8

Three ingredients in this recipe are very important in the South—Bourbon whisky, peaches, and chicken. They combine wonderfully in this dish, which also makes use of a Vidalia onion—a sweet onion grown in the soil around Vidalia, Georgia. If these are not found in your area, any sweet onion variety may be substituted.

2 tablespoons olive oil
2 tablespoons butter
12 whole chicken thighs
1 Vidalia onion, finely chopped
1½ cups Bourbon whiskey
1¼ cups BBQ Sauce, see recipe p. 136, plus
  ¼ cup light brown sugar

1 jar peach preserves
2 tablespoons Worcestershire sauce
4 cloves garlic, peeled
3 whole green onions, sliced for garnish

Preheat the oven to 300 degrees F.
  Heat the olive oil and butter in a heavy, oven-proof saucepan over medium-high heat. Place the chicken thighs, four at a time, in the pot skin-side down. Brown on both sides, then remove to a plate until all the chicken has been browned. Pour off half the grease, and return the pan to the heat and add the onions, stirring, for 2 minutes. Slowly add the whiskey to the pot, being careful not to splash if cooking near an open flame. Continue to cook over medium-high heat for 3 to 4 minutes, stirring frequently, to allow the liquid to

reduce. Scrape the bottom of the pan as you stir. Pour in the barbecue sauce, sugar, peach preserves, ½ cup water, and the Worcestershire sauce. Add the garlic and stir until the sauce is hot and bubbly. Return the chicken to the pot, skin-side up. Cover and bake for 1½ hours.

BBQ Lamb

serves 6 to 8

For the home cook, a lamb shank can easily be prepared in the oven or slow cooker to produce tender results. The key is "low and slow"—using low heat for a long time.

6 tablespoons olive oil, divided
1 (5 to 6-pound) boned sirloin half leg of lamb
10 cloves garlic
3 tablespoons fresh lemon juice
2 tablespoons smoked paprika

2 teaspoons coarse salt
2 teaspoons freshly ground pepper
BBQ Sauce, your choice, see recipes,
  p. 136-137

Heat 3 tablespoons olive oil in a large Dutch oven over medium-high heat. Sear the lamb in the hot pan on all sides, about 2 minutes each side.

Preheat the oven to 250 degrees F.

Remove the lamb from the Dutch oven and use a sharp knife to make 10 small cuts about 1-inch deep over all the roast. Insert a garlic clove into each slit. Brush the lamb with the remaining olive oil and place it in a roasting pan. Sprinkle with lemon juice, paprika, salt, and pepper. Cover and seal with heavy aluminum foil and bake for 6 to 8 hours. A meat thermometer inserted into the thickest point of the meat should read 140 degrees F when done.

Remove the roast from the oven and allow it to rest for 10 minutes before slicing. Serve the lamb sliced, or on a bun with barbecue sauce.

RECOLLECTIONS

Barbecued lamb has been a popular item on the menu since 1936. Lamb is not a meat that is often barbecued in the South; it was specially created for Johnny Harris's Jewish customers. Gail Greene, the food critic, wrote that Johnny Harris's barbecued lamb was the best she'd ever tasted. The restaurant used to buy New Zealand lamb, but now uses domestic. It smokes just like pork.

Slow-cooked BBQ Pork 2

serves 8

1 (2-pound) boneless pork butt roast
2 cups apple juice
1 large Vidalia or sweet onion
4 cloves garlic, minced
1 (18-ounce) bottle Johnny Harris Bar-B-Cue
    Sauce, or BBQ Sauce, see recipe, p. 136

¼ cup melted butter
8 hamburger buns

Preheat a slow cooker or large Dutch oven on low heat. Add the pork roast and pour the apple juice over the top. Sprinkle the onion and garlic over the top and around the sides, cover, and cook on low heat for 6 to 8 hours. When the meat is done, it shreds easily when pulled apart using 2 forks. Pour the bottle of sauce over the shredded meat and mix well. Using a brush, cover insides of buns with melted butter and toast lightly in oven. Serve the meat on toasted buns with pickle slices and Homemade Coleslaw (see recipe, p. 86).

Grilled Flank Steak

serves 6

3 cups dry red wine
3 cups chopped onion
2¼ cups soy sauce
¾ cup olive oil
8 large garlic cloves, chopped

1 tablespoon plus 1½ teaspoons dry mustard
1 tablespoon plus 1½ teaspoons ginger
1 (4.5-pound) flank steak

Combine the first 7 ingredients in a large bowl and mix well. Pour over the steak and turn to coat evenly. Cover and refrigerate for 3 to 6 hours.

  Grill the steak over medium-high heat for 4 minutes on each side for rare, or longer for desired doneness. (The meat will continue to cook slightly after removal from the grill.) Let it rest for 2 minutes, then slice the steak thinly on the diagonal to serve.

Pork Chops with Mustard Gravy

serves 6 to 8

12 (2-pound) boneless pork loin chops,
  thinly sliced
1 teaspoon salt
1 teaspoon black pepper
½ cup plus 3 tablespoons all-purpose flour
3 tablespoons vegetable oil plus
  2 tablespoons, divided

½ cup finely chopped onion
2 cloves garlic, minced
2 cups chicken broth
1 cup heavy cream
½ cup Dijon mustard, or Carolina
  Mustard-Style Sauce, or see recipe, p. 136
2 teaspoons lemon juice

Sprinkle the pork chops with salt and pepper on both sides.

Put ½ cup flour in a shallow dish and dredge the chops, shaking off the excess flour, to lightly coat. In a large skillet over medium-high heat, add enough oil to coat the bottom of the pan. Sear the chops in batches, cooking approximately 2 minutes each side. Remove the pork to a hot plate, or cover to keep warm, while preparing the gravy.

Whisk the remaining 2 tablespoons oil, 3 tablespoons flour, the onions, and garlic into the pan drippings. Whisk over medium heat for 3 minutes, or until the flour is lightly browned. Whisk in the chicken broth and continue to cook, stirring, until the gravy thickens. Reduce the heat to low and add the heavy cream, the mustard (or sauce), and the lemon juice. Return the pork chops to the pan and simmer for 5 more minutes.

Country Steak with Onions and Mushrooms

serves 8

2 pounds ground round beef
½ cup oats
3 teaspoons dry mustard
1 beef bouillon cube, crushed
1 teaspoon Worcestershire sauce
1 tablespoon Johnny Harris Bar-B-Cue sauce,
  or BBQ Sauce, see recipe, p. 136
Salt and pepper to taste
1 tablespoon butter
1 tablespoon olive oil

Sauce
1 large Vidalia or sweet onion, thinly sliced
1½ cups sliced mushrooms
1 teaspoon cornstarch
3 cups beef broth
1 teaspoon Worcestershire sauce
1 tablespoon Johnny Harris Bar-B-Cue
  Sauce, or BBQ Sauce, see recipe, p. 136

Combine the ground beef and oats in a large bowl. In a measuring cup, combine the dry mustard, bouillon, Worcestershire sauce, barbecue sauce, 1 tablespoon water and the salt and pepper, and pour over the beef and oats. Using your hands, mix the beef mixture well and form into 8 patties.

Heat the butter and olive oil in a large skillet over medium-high heat and cook the patties until they are no longer pink. Transfer to a warm plate.

To make the sauce: Reduce the heat of the skillet to medium, add the sliced onions and mushrooms and sauté 5 to 6 minutes, or until tender. In a small cup, mix the cornstarch with 1 tablespoon of the beef broth. Pour the rest of the beef broth into the pan with the mushrooms and onions, and add the cornstarch mixture, the Worcestershire sauce, and the barbecue sauce. Continue to cook over medium heat until the sauce thickens. Top each steak patty with a spoonful of the onions and mushrooms.

Pulled BBQ Chicken Sandwiches

serves 6 to 8

1 ½ teaspoons chili powder
1 ½ teaspoons paprika
½ teaspoon salt
¼ teaspoon cayenne
¼ teaspoon pepper

1 ½ pounds boneless, skinless chicken thighs
1 ½ pounds boneless, skinless chicken breasts
1 ½ cups Johnny Harris Bar-B-Cue Sauce, or
 BBQ Sauce, see recipe, p. 136

Mix the chili powder, paprika, salt, cayenne, and the pepper in a small bowl. Rub this mixture evenly over the chicken pieces and place them in a large Dutch oven or slow cooker. Add ½ cup of the barbeque sauce and stir to coat. Cover and cook over low heat for 4 to 6 hours, or until the chicken is tender. Transfer the cooked chicken to a large bowl, and, using 2 forks, pierce and pull the meat in opposite directions, shredding into 1-inch pieces. Do not shred too thinly.

Skim the fat from the surface of the pan drippings and reserve 1 cup of the liquid. Heat the remaining 1 cup barbeque sauce until hot and add this, with the reserved liquid, to the shredded chicken. Toss thoroughly. Serve on hamburger buns with pickle chips.

Spicy Buttermilk Fried Chicken

serves 6

2 cups all-purpose flour
1/2 teaspoon salt
1/4 teaspoon freshly ground pepper
1 1/2 to 2 teaspoons cayenne
1 teaspoon garlic powder

1/2 teaspoon paprika
1 cup buttermilk
2 1/2 to 3 pounds chicken pieces
Vegetable oil, for frying

In a large bowl, combine the flour, salt, pepper, cayenne, garlic powder, and paprika.

Place the buttermilk in a shallow pie plate. Dredge the chicken in the flour mixture, dip each piece in the buttermilk, and dredge again in the flour mixture.

In a deep Dutch oven, heat 1½ inches vegetable oil to 350 degrees F. Using tongs, carefully add a few pieces of chicken to the oil and fry for 12 to 15 minutes, turning once, until the meat is no longer pink and the crust is golden brown. Drain on paper towels and keep warm in a 300 degree F oven while frying the remaining pieces.

Famous Batterless Fried Chicken

serves 4 to 6

Battered chicken is usually fried at 325 F to prevent the batter from burning before the chicken is done on the inside. This higher temperature will help crisp up the skin as the chicken cooks.

2 whole chickens, cut up, with skin on
64 ounces (2 quarts) peanut oil
Salt and pepper to taste

Wash the chicken pieces thoroughly under cold water, then drain on paper towels for about 10 to 15 minutes. Pat each piece totally dry. (This step is important—any water left on the chicken will cause the grease to splatter when dropped into the hot oil.)

In a large pot or electric fryer, heat the peanut oil to 350 degrees F. Gently ease the chicken pieces into the oil, using the larger pieces first. Fry for 14 to 20 minutes. (Smaller pieces like legs and wings take 14 minutes, while larger thighs and breasts take 20 minutes.) The chicken will be done when the skin turns a nice golden brown. Use a slotted spoon or tongs to remove the chicken and drain on paper towels. Sprinkle with salt and pepper to taste and serve immediately.

Chicken Pot Pie

yields 2 pies

1 cup chopped celery
1 cup chopped sweet onion
4 tablespoons butter
4 cups chicken stock, divided
3 cups diced, cooked chicken
1 cup petit pois

1 cup diced carrots
4 tablespoons cornstarch
2 cups fresh baby spinach leaves
¾ teaspoon freshly ground pepper
2 (10-inch) pie crust pastry

Preheat the oven to 350 degrees F.

In a medium saucepan over medium heat, sauté the celery and onion in the butter for 3 to 5 minutes, until tender. Add 3 cups chicken stock, the chicken, petit pois, and carrots and cook, uncovered, for 5 minutes, stirring occasionally. Combine the cornstarch and remaining chicken stock and add to the saucepan. Increase the heat to high and cook, stirring constantly, for 2 minutes until the sauce thickens and becomes bubbly. Add the spinach leaves and pepper and cook 1 more minute until the spinach is wilted. Divide and pour into 2 ungreased 10-inch pie plates.

Roll out the pastry doughs and place 1 over each pie plate. Trim any overlap around the edges and cut 5 (1-inch) slits in each top to allow steam to escape. Bake for 45 to 55 minutes, or until the crust is lightly browned. Let stand for 5 minutes before serving.

Baked Lemon Chicken with Mushroom Sauce

serves 6

1 tablespoon olive oil
6 skinless, boneless chicken breast halves
1 lemon
¼ cup butter

3 cups sliced fresh mushrooms
2 tablespoons all-purpose flour
¾ cup chicken broth
1 tablespoon chopped fresh parsley

Preheat the oven to 400 degrees F.

Pour the olive oil in a 9 x 9-inch glass baking dish. Place the chicken breasts in the dish and turn to coat each side with oil. Squeeze the juice of ½ lemon over the top. Slice the rest into thin rounds to cover the tops of the chicken breasts. Bake for 30 to 40 minutes, or until lightly browned.

In a large skillet over medium heat, melt the butter and cook the sliced mushrooms for 6 minutes, stirring constantly, until they are tender and browned. Sprinkle with the flour and stir to blend well. Add the chicken broth and continue to stir until the sauce is thick and creamy. Spoon over the chicken breasts before serving and garnish with the chopped parsley.

Stuffed Pork Chops

serves 6 to 8

4 tablespoons olive oil, divided
4 cloves garlic, minced
12 sundried tomatoes, diced
2 (10-ounce) bag frozen spinach, thawed
   and squeezed dry
1 teaspoon salt
Freshly ground pepper
½ teaspoon dried thyme

½ cup goat cheese
⅔ cup cream cheese
8 (4-ounce) center-cut pork chops
3 cups chicken broth
Zest of 1 lemon
4 tablespoons lemon juice
4 teaspoons Dijon mustard

Heat 2 tablespoons olive oil in a medium sauté pan over medium heat, add the garlic and cook for 1 minute, then add the tomatoes, spinach, salt, pepper, and thyme. Stir to combine and cook another 2 minutes. Transfer the mixture to a medium bowl and stir in the goat cheese and cream cheese. Set aside.

With a sharp knife, cut a pocket in each pork chop and stuff the chop with ⅛ of the spinach/tomato mixture, then pinch the meat pocket closed. Season with salt and pepper.

In a small bowl, combine the chicken broth, lemon zest, lemon juice, and mustard.

Heat the remaining 2 tablespoons olive oil in a large heavy skillet over medium-high heat. Cook the pork chops, 4 at a time, for 4 minutes per side, or until golden brown. Transfer the chops to a warm baking dish and cover to keep hot.

Cook the chicken broth mixture in the skillet over medium-high heat, scraping up the brown bits from the bottom of the pan as the broth simmers. Cook for 8 minutes, or until the broth is reduced by half. Spoon the sauce over the pork before serving.

Ribeye Steaks with Blue Cheese Butter

serves 4

½ cup crumbled blue cheese
½ cup (1 stick) butter, softened
¼ cup walnuts, toasted
2 tablespoons minced fresh parsley
1¾ teaspoons minced fresh rosemary

6 large cloves garlic , peeled
½ teaspoon salt
½ teaspoon pepper
4 (12-ounce) beef ribeye steaks

In a small bowl, combine the blue cheese, butter, walnuts, parsley, and ¾ teaspoon rosemary. Mix well, shape into a 5-inch long log, and wrap in plastic wrap. Refrigerate for 30 minutes, or until firm.

In a food processor, combine the garlic, salt, pepper, and the remaining rosemary and process until well blended. Rub the garlic mixture over both sides of the steaks.

Grill the steaks on a covered grill over medium heat for 4 to 6 minutes on each side for rare, or until the meat reaches the desired doneness.

Unwrap the blue cheese butter, cut four ½-inch pats butter and place 1 pat atop each steak. Serve immediately and pass or refrigerate the remaining butter.

Harris's Mouth-Watering Meat Loaf

yields 1 loaf

2 pounds ground beef
1 pound ground pork sausage, mild
½ cup sweet onion, chopped
1 cup Johnny Harris Bar-B-Cue Sauce,
  or any flavor sauce, see recipes, pp. 136-137

1/3 cup green bell pepper, chopped
1 cup crushed saltines
2 eggs, lightly beaten
½ cup brown sugar

Preheat the oven to 350 degrees F.

Gently mix the ground beef, sausage, onion, ⅔ cup barbecue sauce, bell pepper, saltines, eggs, and ¼ cup brown sugar. Form into a loaf, place in a lightly-greased loaf pan, and bake for 1 hour.

Mix the remaining ¼ cup brown sugar and ⅓ cup sauce, pour over the meatloaf, and bake an additional 15 minutes. An internal meat thermometer should read 160 degrees F when the meat is done. Let stand for 20 minutes at room temperature before slicing.

Sweet and Spicy Short Ribs

serves 8

8 pounds beef chuck short ribs
1 cup ketchup
1 cup Johnny Harris Bar-B-Cue Sauce, or BBQ
 Sauce, see recipe, p. 136
1 cup Steak Sauce, see recipe p. 137

2 tablespoons sugar
2 tablespoons horseradish
2 teaspoons salt
4 medium onions, sliced

In a large Dutch oven or slow cooker, combine 2 cups water with all the ingredients except the onions. Bring to a boil, then reduce the heat to low, cover, and simmer for 2 to 3 hours, or until the meat is very tender. Let cool, then refrigerate several hours. Any fat congealed on the top after chilling should be skimmed off with a large serving spoon.

Preheat the oven to 350 degrees F.

Transfer the short ribs to a large baking dish, reserving the sauce. Discard any loose bones and arrange the sliced onions over the short ribs, then pour the sauce over all. Cover with foil and bake for 30 minutes.

Bourbon-Glazed Ham

serves 10 to 12

1 (5-pound) ham, boneless
1/3 cup Bourbon whiskey
½ cup brown sugar
1 (8-ounce) can crushed pineapple with juice

½ cup honey
3 cloves garlic, minced

Score the fatty surface of the ham with a sharp knife in a diagonal pattern, making ½-inch deep slices. Place the ham in a large, zip-top bag and add the whiskey, brown sugar, crushed pineapple with juice, the honey, garlic, and ¾ cup water to the bag. Refrigerate at least 8 hours and turn the bag over every 2 hours to make sure the marinade evenly coats all sides.

Preheat the oven to 350 degrees F.

Transfer the ham and the marinade to a large baking dish and bake for 1½ to 2 hours, or until a meat thermometer reaches 165 degrees F. Baste every 20 to 30 minutes using the sauce in the pan. Slice and serve immediately.

Chicken and Dumplings

serves 4 to 6

1 whole chicken, skin-on
1 large onion, peeled and quartered
3 carrots, cut into 3-inch pieces
3 stalks celery, cut into 3-inch pieces
Salt and pepper to taste

Dumplings
3 cups all-purpose flour
¾ teaspoon baking soda
¾ teaspoon salt
4½ tablespoons shortening
1 cup milk

Place the chicken in a large stock pot with enough water to cover by 1 to 2 inches. Add the onion, carrots, and celery and bring the pot to a boil, then reduce the heat to low and simmer for 1 hour.

When the chicken is done, remove it from the broth and allow it to cool enough to handle. Remove the skin and bones and discard. Place the chicken meat in a bowl and shred into bite-sized pieces. Set aside.

Strain the broth into a large bowl, discarding the vegetables. Remove 6 cups of the broth and return this to the stock pot. The remainder of the broth may be frozen for use later.

To make the dumplings: Mix the flour, baking soda, and salt together in a bowl. Cut the shortening into the flour mixture using a fork or pastry cutter, until the dough resembles small peas. Add the milk, ¼ cup at a time, until the dough begins to form a ball. You may not need to use the entire cup. Roll the dough out on a lightly floured surface to ¼- to ½-inch thick. (The dough does not have to be uniform in thickness.)

Using a sharp knife, cut the dough into 1 x 3-inch pieces. Allow the dumplings to sit about 30 minutes to harden a little.

Turn the heat to medium-low on the stock pot and bring the broth to a gentle simmer. Drop the dumplings in the simmering broth 2 or 3 at a time, stirring so they do not stick together, until all the dumplings are used. Reduce the heat to low, add the chicken, and cook for 20 to 25 minutes, until the broth thickens. Season with the salt and pepper to taste.

Chicken with Blackberry Mustard Cream

serves 6

3 tablespoons olive oil
6 boneless, skinless chicken breasts
1 shallot, minced
1 teaspoon minced garlic
½ cup whole grain mustard
¼ cup blackberry jam

2 cups heavy whipping cream
1 teaspoon salt
½ teaspoon garlic powder
¼ teaspoon freshly ground pepper
Fresh blackberries, for garnish

In a large skillet, heat the olive oil over medium heat.

Using a meat mallet, pound the chicken breasts to ½-inch thick, and cook in the hot oil for 3 to 4 minutes on each side, or until lightly browned. Remove the chicken and set aside, reserving the drippings in the skillet. Cook the shallot and garlic in the drippings for 2 minutes, stirring constantly. Add the mustard and blackberry jam, stirring until the jam melts, then add the cream, salt, garlic powder, and pepper, and stir to combine. Return the chicken breasts to the pan, reduce the heat to medium-low, and simmer uncovered for 20 minutes, turning occasionally, or until the chicken is tender and the sauce has slightly thickened. Place the chicken breasts on individual plates and spoon the sauce over each serving. Garnish with fresh berries before serving.

RECOLLECTIONS

There are 21 booths in the main dining room. Each one is completely separate and built from floor to ceiling with tongue-n-groove pine paneling, stained cherry. The 7-foot-long tables seat 6 comfortably. There is no #13 booth, as Red Donaldson was superstitious of unlucky numbers. That booth is #00, a double zero. Each booth has a service button which, when pushed, illuminates a light on the outside of the booth to alert the servers that a guest needs attention. During Prohibition, the booths were equipped with curtains. Guests would bring their liquor in brown paper bags and close the curtains while they poured. The curtains are no longer used, but the buttons are still a popular feature.

Seafood

Savannah Blue Crab Cakes with Lemon Aioli

serves 8

2 large eggs
½ cup onion, chopped
½ cup green pepper, chopped
½ cup red pepper, chopped
3 tablespoons white wine
1 tablespoon lemon juice
1 teaspoon Worcestershire sauce
1 teaspoon dry mustard
½ to 1 teaspoon cayenne
1 pound lump crabmeat
1½ cups Panko breadcrumbs
2 tablespoons butter
2 tablespoons olive oil
Lemon slices, for garnish

Lemon Aioli
½ cup mayonnaise
1 clove garlic, finely minced
1 tablespoon chopped fresh chives
3 tablespoons fresh lemon juice
½ teaspoon lemon zest
Salt to taste
Freshly ground black pepper to taste

Combine the first 9 ingredients in a large bowl. Mix well, then gently stir in the crabmeat and ¾ cup Panko, taking care to leave the larger pieces of crabmeat intact. Divide and shape the crabmeat mixture into 8 patties.

Place the remaining Panko in a shallow bowl and dredge the patties to evenly coat each side.

Heat the butter and olive oil in a medium skillet over medium heat, and sauté the patties, 4 at a time, for 3 to 4 minutes per side, until both sides are golden brown. Transfer the crab cakes from the pan to drain on paper towels. Serve hot with a dollop of lemon aioli.

To make the lemon aioli: Mix all the ingredients together in a small bowl. Use immediately, or cover tightly and refrigerate until ready to use.

Fried Oysters

serves 6 to 8

1 cup yellow cornmeal
½ cup Panko breadcrumbs
1 teaspoon freshly ground pepper
¼ teaspoon sweet paprika
¼ teaspoon cayenne

Salt to taste
4 dozen fresh oysters, shucked and drained
½ cup (1 stick) butter, melted
Peanut oil, for frying
Tartar sauce, your choice brand

In a shallow pie plate, combine the cornmeal, Panko, pepper, paprika, cayenne, and salt and mix well. Dip the oysters quickly in the butter then dredge lightly in the cornmeal mixture and place them on a large platter.

Fill a large heavy skillet 1 inch full with peanut oil, and heat to 375 degrees F. Use a thermometer to test the heat, or toss a small piece of bread into the pan—if it sizzles quickly, the oil is ready. Drop the oysters a few at a time into the hot oil and fry for no more than 2 minutes until golden brown, turning once. Use tongs or a slotted spoon to remove and drain on paper towels. Make sure the oil comes back up to temperature between batches to prevent sogginess. Serve hot with tartar sauce.

RECOLLECTIONS

It's nice to go where everyone knows you. It seems like every important milestone in life is celebrated at Johnny Harris's—birthdays, engagements, confirmations, weddings, and funerals. When I was little, my parents put me and my siblings in the kitchen while they were in the bar, and paid the waiters to give us cherry Cokes. At 17, I was finally old enough to go dancing at the restaurant, and I remember that Mr. Pennwaller danced with me all evening and bought me pink daiquiris. Now that I'm semi-retired, I go to Johnny Harris's for lunch after noon mass each Monday with a group of Catholic women friends. We enjoy each other's company and sometimes stay until three in the afternoon—when it's time for cocktails!

My business, Destination Management, gives motorcoach tours, and one of the tours from Victory Drive out to Isle of Hope includes, of course, Johnny Harris restaurant. —Pat Tuttle

Southern Fried Catfish

serves 8

1 1/2 cups buttermilk
1/2 teaspoon Frank's Red-Hot Cayenne Pepper
  Sauce, or your choice brand
8 (6-ounce) catfish fillets
1/3 cup stone-ground yellow cornmeal
1/3 cup corn flour
1/3 cup all-purpose flour

2 teaspoons salt
1 teaspoon ground black pepper
1 teaspoon ground red pepper
1/4 teaspoon garlic powder
Peanut oil, for frying

Whisk together the buttermilk and hot sauce. Place the catfish in a single layer in a 13 x 9-inch baking dish, and pour the buttermilk mixture over the fish. Cover and refrigerate for 8 hours, turning once.

When you are ready to cook, stir together the cornmeal, both flours, the salt, black pepper, red pepper, and garlic powder in a shallow pie plate. Let the fish stand at room temperature for 10 minutes and then remove from the buttermilk mixture and let any excess liquid drain off. Dredge the fillets in the cornmeal mixture and shake off the excess.

Fill a deep cast-iron, or heavy duty, skillet with at least 2 inches of oil and heat to 360 degrees F. Use a thermometer to test the heat, or toss a small piece of bread in the pan—if it sizzles quickly, the oil is ready. Fry the fish in batches for 2 minutes on each side, or until golden brown. Transfer the fish to a pan lined with paper towels, cover with foil, and keep them warm in a 225 degree F oven until ready to serve.

Sweet & Spicy Honey Barbecue Salmon

serves 6

½ cup Johnny Harris Bar-B-Cue Sauce, or
  BBQ Sauce, see recipe, p. 136
2 tablespoons brown sugar, or substitute
  Johnny Harris Spicy Honey BBQ Sauce,
  see recipe, p. 137
1 green onion, chopped

4 fresh salmon fillets (1 pound total weight)

Spinach
1 tablespoon olive oil
1 clove garlic , minced
1 (10-ounce) bag baby spinach leaves

In a small bowl, combine the barbecue sauce with the brown sugar (or Spicy Honey BBQ Sauce), and green onion. Set aside.

Heat a grill to medium-high and grease the rack with vegetable oil. Grill the fillets for 4 minutes on each side, turning once, and brush with the honey sauce generously after each turn. The fish is done when the flesh flakes easily with a fork. Serve hot over a bed of sautéed spinach.

To prepare the spinach: Heat the olive oil in large skillet over medium-high heat and cook the garlic for 2 minutes, then add the spinach, cover, and cook 6 to 8 minutes more, stirring occasionally.

Maple-Glazed Salmon

serves 8

½ cup red grapefruit juice
4 tablespoons balsamic vinegar
4 tablespoons maple syrup
4 garlic cloves, minced

4 teaspoons olive oil
8 salmon fillets
½ teaspoon salt
½ teaspoon pepper

In a small saucepan over high heat, bring the grapefruit juice, vinegar, maple syrup, and garlic to a boil. Reduce the heat and simmer, uncovered, for 5 minutes. Transfer 4 tablespoons to a small bowl, and add the oil. Set the remaining glaze aside.

Sprinkle the salmon fillets with salt and pepper. Moisten a paper towel with oil and lightly coat a grill rack. Place the fillets skin-side down on the grill, cover, and cook over medium heat, basting occasionally with the maple glaze, for 10 to 12 minutes or until the fish flakes easily with a fork. Remove and drizzle with the remaining glaze before serving.

Crabmeat Au Gratin

serves 6 to 8

1 ½ sticks butter
¾ cup flour
1 ½ teaspoons salt
1 teaspoon white pepper
1 teaspoon paprika
6 cups half-and-half

3 ½ cups sharp cheddar cheese, grated
2 tablespoons Worcestershire sauce
5 tablespoons dry sherry
6 cups lump crabmeat, picked over for shells
½ cup Panko breadcrumbs
½ cup grated Parmesan cheese

Preheat the oven to 325 degrees F.

Melt the butter in a saucepan over medium heat. Stir in the flour, salt, white pepper, and paprika, and gradually pour in the half-and-half, stirring constantly, until the sauce is smooth and creamy. Reduce the heat to medium-low, sprinkle in 3 cups cheddar cheese, and stir until the cheese melts into the sauce. Add the Worcestershire sauce, sherry, and crabmeat. Using a spatula, gently stir to blend, taking care not to break up the lumps of crabmeat.

Pour the crabmeat mixture into a well-greased 2 ½- to 3-quart casserole dish.

In a small bowl, mix the last ½ cup cheddar cheese, the Panko breadcrumbs, and Parmesan cheese. Sprinkle evenly over the top of the crabmeat mixture and bake for 20 to 25 minutes, until the top is golden brown and the edges are bubbling.

Traditional Oyster Dressing

serves 12 to 16

My grandmother, Maude Donaldson, always put out a big spread of home-cooked favorites for the holidays. Ham, rice and gravy, butterbeans, green beans, Ambrosia, pound cake, and a big turkey, to name just a few of her treats. The table would not be complete without her homemade oyster dressing. She usually made a large pan, half with and half without oysters.

3 cups dry cornbread, cut into cubes
3 cups dry white bread, cut into cubes
4 tablespoons butter
1 cup onions, finely chopped
3 cloves garlic, minced
1 cup celery, chopped
1 dozen oysters, canned or fresh

2 eggs
½ teaspoon ground sage
½ teaspoon salt
¼ teaspoon pepper
2 eggs, hardboiled, peeled and chopped
2 to 3 cups chicken broth

Spread the cubed cornbread and white bread out onto a large baking sheet and let it sit uncovered overnight, or heat in a warm oven for 1 hour to dry out the bread. When ready to assemble the dressing, place the bread in a large mixing bowl and set aside.

Preheat the oven to 350 degrees F.

In a large skillet over medium heat, melt the butter and sauté the onions, garlic, and celery for 5 to 7 minutes, or until they are soft. Add the oysters and stir for about 5 minutes. Remove the skillet from the heat and, using a pair of kitchen shears, roughly chop the oysters into bite-size pieces. Pour the sautéed vegetables and oysters from the skillet into the bowl with the bread cubes.

Crack the 2 eggs in one side of the bowl and add the sage, salt, and pepper on top of the eggs. Use your hand to gently fold all ingredients together. Add the chopped hard-boiled eggs and fold in. Add the chicken broth, ½ cup at a time, and gently stir until the desired moisture level is achieved.

Pour the dressing into a lightly-greased 10 x 13-inch casserole dish and bake uncovered for 35 to 45 minutes, or until the top is golden brown. Serve roast with turkey or other game birds.

Low Country Boil

serves 12

1 ½ cups Seafood Seasoning, see recipe, p.138
2 pounds red new potatoes
2 large Vidalia or sweet onions, peeled and
  quartered
12 ears of corn, husked, cleaned and halved

3 pounds smoked beef sausage, cut into
  1 ½ -inch pieces
4 pounds large fresh shrimp, heads removed,
  shells on
Cocktail sauce or melted butter, for dipping

Bring 6 quarts water and 1 cup Seafood Seasoning to a boil in a large stock pot. Add the potatoes and boil for 5 minutes, then add the onions and corn and cook for another 15 minutes. Add the sausage and shrimp and cook for 5 more minutes, or until the shrimp turn pink. Drain immediately and pour onto a table covered with newspaper, or serve in a big bowl. Sprinkle with the remaining ½ cup Seafood Seasoning. Serve with cocktail sauce and melted butter for dipping.

Flounder in Brown Butter Wine Sauce

serves 6

½ cup all-purpose flour
½ teaspoon salt
½ teaspoon pepper
6 flounder fillets

1 ½ sticks (12 tablespoons) butter, divided
2 cloves garlic, minced
¼ cup dry white wine
1 tablespoon capers

In a shallow dish, combine the flour, salt, and pepper. Dredge the fillets in the flour mixture to coat.

In a large skillet, melt 2 tablespoons butter over medium heat and cook 3 fillets for 3 to 4 minutes per side, or until the fish flakes easily with a fork. Repeat using another 2 tablespoons butter for each remaining fillet. Covered with foil and hold the cooked fish in a warm oven.

Add the remaining ½ cup butter to the skillet and cook for 2 minutes over medium heat. Add the minced garlic and cook another 2 minutes, or until the butter is lightly browned, then add the wine and cook for 1 more minute. Stir in the capers, and return the fish to the hot skillet. Spoon the sauce over the fish and serve immediately.

Chatham Deviled Crab

serves 8

8 tablespoons (1 stick) butter
2/3 cup minced sweet onion
1 cup heavy cream
4 tablespoons sweet sherry
2 teaspoons minced fresh chives
1 teaspoon cayenne

2 teaspoons dry mustard
1 teaspoon Worcestershire sauce
Salt and pepper to taste
1 pound fresh claw crabmeat
4 large egg yolks, slightly beaten
1/2 cup dry bread crumbs

Preheat the oven to 425 degrees F.

In a medium skillet over medium heat, melt 4 tablespoons butter and add the onion. Cook for 2 minutes, stirring constantly, until the onion softens. Add the heavy cream, sherry, chives, cayenne, dry mustard, Worcestershire sauce, salt, and pepper and cook for 2 to 3 more minutes. Stir in the crabmeat, remove the skillet from the heat, and stir in the egg yolks until well blended.

Divide the mixture between 8 individual baking dishes, ramekins or blue crab shells and sprinkle each with 1 tablespoon breadcrumbs. Dot with the remaining 4 tablespoons butter and bake for 10 minutes, or until the breadcrumbs are a golden brown and the mixture is hot and bubbly. Serve hot.

Tomato Basil Grouper

serves 6

¾ cup olive oil
3 Roma tomatoes, seeded and chopped
¼ cup balsamic vinegar
4 cloves garlic, minced

¼ cup minced fresh basil
1 teaspoon cayenne
5 pounds grouper fillets (or a firm white fish suitable for grilling)

Combine the oil, tomatoes, balsamic vinegar, garlic, and basil in a medium bowl, and mix well. Reserve ½ cup of the marinade and set aside. Place the grouper fillets in a large zip-top bag, pour the remaining marinade over the fish, and seal the bag. Massage the marinade to completely cover the fillets, and refrigerate for 1 hour.

Remove the fillets from the bag and allow them to come to room temperature. Preheat the grill to medium heat, and grill the fillets until the center of each fish is opaque and the flesh flakes easily with a fork. Spoon the reserved marinade over each fillet and serve immediately.

Baked Lobster Savannah

serves 8

½ cup (1 stick) butter
½ cup flour
4 cups milk
4 egg yolks, beaten
½ cup dry sherry, or white wine
2 cups chopped fresh mushrooms
1 green pepper, diced

4 cups chopped cooked lobster meat
3 tablespoons finely chopped pimentos
4 teaspoons paprika
Salt and pepper to taste
1 cup Panko breadcrumbs
1 cup grated Parmesan cheese

Melt the butter in a small saucepan over medium heat and gradually stir in the flour, eliminating any lumps. Add the milk slowly, stirring until the sauce thickens. Stir a little of the thickened sauce into the beaten egg yolks, then add this back into the saucepan. Add the sherry, mushrooms, and green pepper and cook over medium heat, stirring constantly, for 15 minutes. Remove from the heat and add the lobster meat, pimentos, paprika, salt, and pepper. Pour the mixture into a well-greased, 3½-quart casserole dish. Sprinkle with the Panko breadcrumbs and Parmesan cheese and bake at 375 degrees F for 30 minutes. Serve hot.

Garlic Shrimp

serves 6

3 pounds (32 count) shrimp, peeled and
 deveined
½ cup olive oil
¼ cup chopped parsley
8 cloves garlic, minced
1½ teaspoons crushed red pepper flakes

½ teaspoon fresh ground black pepper
½ cup (1 stick) butter, melted
1 cup Panko breadcrumbs
1 cup freshly grated Parmesan cheese

Preheat the oven to 300 degrees F.

Arrange the shrimp on a sheet pan. Pour the olive oil over the shrimp.

Combine the parsley, garlic, the red pepper flakes, and black pepper and sprinkle over the shrimp. Cover with a sheet of aluminum foil and bake for 15 minutes. Turn the shrimp over and drizzle with the butter, then sprinkle with the Panko breadcrumbs and Parmesan cheese. Bake uncovered for 5 to 10 more minutes, until the breadcrumbs are golden brown and the shrimp are pink.

 **RECOLLECTIONS**

Celebrities started coming to Johnny Harris's during WWII, when Hunter Airfield was fogged in. Bob Hope's crew who entertained the troups came into the restaurant and stayed all evening until the planes were flying again. The group included Bob Hope, Jerry Callona, the actress Frances Langford, and the guitarist Tony Romero.

A local promoter, Buster White, brought movie stars in during the 1950s, and a lady from the Chamber of Commerce brought Red Skelton, the comedian, in the 1960s. He loved the barbecue ribs, and wrote on the menu, "Thanks for the Ribbing."

The comedian Jackie Gleason came by yacht to Hilton Head to visit and ordered 100 pounds of ribs sent over just for himself. After that, when he traveled to Miami by train, he had someone come by to get him a pile of ribs for the trip.

Other celebrity guests include Savannah native songwriter Johnny Mercer, who always ate in the Kitchen; John Berendt, who wrote Midnight in the Garden of Good and Evil; *Clint Eastswood; Robert Duvall; Michael Douglass, and many others.*

Sweet Potato Encrusted Grouper

serves 8

1 cup all-purpose flour
Salt and pepper to taste
4 eggs, lightly beaten
1½ pounds (4 medium) sweet potatoes,
    peeled and finely grated

Peanut oil for frying
8 (6 to 8-ounce) grouper fillets
1 tablespoon olive oil
2 (1-pound) packages baby spinach leaves

Using 3 shallow pie pans, place the flour, salt and pepper in the first pan and set aside. In the second pan, pour the beaten eggs. Place the grated sweet potatoes into the third pan.

    Heat a large sauté pan over medium heat and add the enough oil to cover the bottom of the pan, ¼-inch deep. Dip the fish fillets first into the flour mixture, then into the egg, and lastly into the grated sweet potatoes. Place the fillets into the hot pan and sauté for 3 to 4 minutes on each side, or until the fish is thoroughly cooked and flakes easily.

    In a separate sauté pan, heat 1 tablespoon olive oil over medium heat. Layer the spinach leaves in the pan and gently stir until the leaves have wilted, adding more spinach as room allows. Season with salt and pepper.

    To serve, place a portion of the sautéed spinach on the center of each plate and layer the encrusted grouper on top.

Michael Douglas

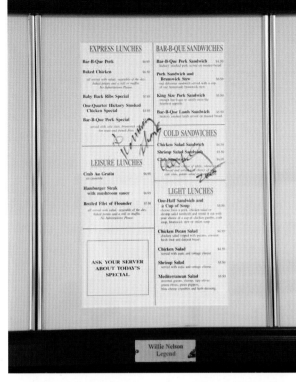

Willie Nelson
Legend

Robert Duvall
Actor

Clint Eastwood
Actor

Dilled Salmon Cakes

serves 8

1 (14.75-ounce) can pink salmon, drained,
  or 4 cooked salmon fillets, skin removed
¾ cup uncooked oats
⅓ cup milk
2 egg whites, lightly beaten
2 tablespoons chopped onion
1 teaspoon dried dill weed
¼ teaspoon salt

Dill Sauce
¾ cup plain yogurt
⅓ cup chopped tomato
⅓ cup chopped cucumber
1 tablespoon chopped onion
1 teaspoon dried dill weed

Combine the salmon, the uncooked oats, milk, egg whites, onion, dill, and salt and mix well. Let stand for 5 minutes, then shape the salmon mixture into 8 patties, each about ½-inch thick. Lightly grease a medium skillet and cook the salmon cakes over medium heat for 3 to 4 minutes on each side until golden brown. Serve hot with the dill sauce.

To make the dill sauce: Combine the ingredients for the sauce in a small bowl and mix well. Spoon a large dollop over each salmon cake just before serving.

Desserts

Coconut Cream Pie

yields 1 (9-inch) pie

Coconut Cream Pie has been a staple at Johnny Harris's as long as I can remember. When I was a child, Ola Mae, our pastry cook, would make scores of them each week. Now this duty is fulfilled by Joanne Polite.

1 Best Pie Crust, see recipe p. 185
¾ cup plus 2 tablespoons sugar
3 cups whole milk
4 eggs, separated
¼ cup cornstarch
1⅓ cups sweetened, flaked coconut

1 teaspoon vanilla
1 tablespoon butter, melted
1 cup whipped cream,
¼ cup toasted coconut

Prepare a pie crust and freeze it for 30 minutes to firm. Preheat an oven to 350 degrees F. Line the crust with parchment paper or aluminum foil, fill with pie weights or dried beans, and bake for 20 minutes.

Remove the pie weights and foil, prick the bottom of the crust with a fork 8 times, then return the crust to the oven for an additional 10 minutes, until golden. Allow to cool completely before filling.

In a non-stick saucepan over high heat, combine ¾ cup sugar and 2¾ cups milk, bring just to a boil to scald the milk, then remove the pan from the heat.

In a small mixing bowl, whisk the remaining milk, egg yolks, and cornstarch until smooth. Temper the egg mixture into the scalded milk. Bring the pan to a boil again and cook for 3 minutes, stirring constantly, until the mixture thickens. Remove the pan from the heat and stir in 1 cup flaked coconut, the vanilla, and the butter. Pour the filling into the prebaked pie crust, cover with plastic wrap, and refrigerate for at least 2 hours.

Heat the oven to 350 degrees F.

Using an electric mixer, beat the egg whites with the remaining 2 tablespoons sugar until stiff peaks form. Spread the meringue evenly over the top of the pie, and sprinkle with the remaining flaked coconut. Bake for 8 to 10 minutes, until the top is golden. Spread the whipped cream over the meringue and garnish with the toasted coconut.

RECOLLECTIONS

Our Coconut Cream pie is so popular that then minister at Aldersgate Methodist church—Jerry Hester, who was a good customer—once preached a sermon about it, called "Liking Coconut Cream Pie."

Fresh Georgia Peach Pie

serves 8

1 Best Pie Crust, prebaked, see recipe p. 185
1 (8-ounce) package cream cheese, room
  temperature
¾ cup sugar
¼ cup fresh orange juice
3 tablespoons fresh lemon juice
6 tablespoons cornstarch
6 cups firm, ripe peaches, peeled, pitted
  and sliced

Praline Sauce
1 stick unsalted butter
½ cup heavy cream
½ cup light brown sugar
⅓ cup toasted pecans, chopped

Prepare the pie crust and freeze it for 30 minutes to firm.

Preheat the oven to 350 degrees F.

Line the pie crust with parchment paper or aluminum foil and fill with pie weights or dried beans, then bake for 20 minutes.

Remove the pie weights and foil, and prick the bottom of the crust with a fork 8 times, then return the crust to the oven for an additional 10 minutes, or until golden. Allow to cool completely before filling.

Mix together the cream cheese and ½ cup sugar in a small bowl and spread the mixture over the bottom of the cooled pie crust.

Place the remaining sugar, orange juice, 2 tablespoons lemon juice, cornstarch, and ½ cup peaches in a blender and puree until smooth.

In another bowl, toss the remaining peaches with 1 tablespoon lemon juice and set aside.

Heat the peach puree in a small saucepan over medium heat until thickened. Add the fresh peaches, stir well to coat, and let the mixture cool. Spread the cooled peaches over the piecrust and refrigerate for 3 hours before serving. Serve with the praline sauce on the side.

To make the praline sauce: Melt the butter, cream, and brown sugar in a small heavy saucepan over medium-high heat. Bring to a boil, then reduce the heat to low. Add the chopped pecans and simmer for 5 minutes, or until the sugar has dissolved and the sauce thickens.

Butter Rum Pound Cake

serves 8 to 10

3 cups all-purpose flour
1½ cups sugar
2 teaspoons baking powder
½ teaspoon baking soda
½ teaspoon salt
4 large eggs, room temperature
1½ cups unsalted butter, room temperature
¾ cup dark rum
2 tablespoons finely grated lemon zest

2 teaspoons vanilla extract
1 cup heavy cream

Rum Glaze
1 cup sugar
⅛ teaspoon salt
1 stick unsalted butter, cubed
½ cup dark rum
Powdered sugar

Preheat oven to 325 degrees F.

In a large bowl, whisk together the flour, sugar, baking powder, baking soda, and salt. Add the eggs, butter, rum, lemon zest, and vanilla to the flour mixture. With an electric mixer on medium speed, beat for 1 minute until well blended. Use a spatula to scrape the sides and bottom of the bowl and continue beating for another 2 minutes. Add the cream and beat on low speed for 30 to 45 seconds until just blended.

Grease a 10-inch tube or Bundt pan with butter, lightly sprinkle with flour, and spread the batter evenly into it. Bake for 65 to 75 minutes (if using a light-colored pan, bake 90 minutes), or until a thin skewer inserted into the center comes out clean. After removing the cake from the oven, transfer the pan to a wire rack to cool while preparing the rum glaze.

To prepare the rum glaze: In a medium saucepan, combine the sugar, salt, butter, and rum and bring to a boil over medium-high heat. Continue to boil, stirring continuously, for 2 minutes, or until the sugar dissolves. Remove from heat and let cool for 5 minutes.

With the cake still warm in the pan, poke holes in the top with a skewer. Pour half the warm rum glaze over the top of the cake. Wait 15 to 20 minutes, then invert the cake onto a platter. Brush the remaining glaze over the cake until absorbed, and allow the cake to cool completely. Dust with powdered sugar before serving.

Carolina Trifle

serves 6 to 8

1 pint heavy cream, whipped
¼ cup sherry
1 loaf pound cake, or Maudie Belle's Sour
  Cream Pound Cake, see recipe, p. 194
Maraschino cherries, for garnish

Custard
4 cups whole milk
6 egg yolks
½ cup sugar

Pour the heavy cream into a medium bowl and beat well until stiff, then fold in 1 table-spoon sherry. Set aside. Cut the pound cake into ½-inch thick slices and place one layer at the bottom of a round glass serving dish.

To make the custard: Heat milk in a saucepan over medium-high heat until mixture begins to steam. Do not boil. In a small bowl, lightly beat the egg yolks and sugar. Pour into in the top of a double boiler, then pour the hot milk over the eggs, a little at a time. Cook over boiling water until the mixture is thick enough to coat a spoon, then remove from the heat and let cool completely. Stir in the remaining sherry.

Spread a layer of the custard over the pound cake layer, and add a layer of whipped cream over that. Repeat the layers until all of the cake slices have been used. Top with a layer of the whipped cream and refrigerate overnight, or at least 8 hours. Spoon into individual dishes and top each with a cherry.

The Best Pie Crust

yields 1 pie crust

½ cup vegetable shortening
1½ cups all-purpose flour

½ teaspoon salt

Using a fork or pastry cutter, mix the shortening, flour, and salt together until the dough is crumbly. Add ½ cup ice water, or enough to just hold the dough together, and mix lightly with a fork. Place on a floured pastry cloth and roll out gently to form a circle 1 inch larger in circumference than the pie plate. Invert a pie plate on top of the rolled-out crust, and, holding the edges of the cloth, flip the plate over carefully. Peel the cloth off and press the dough into the pie plate. Trim off any excess dough, and pinch the edges to form a decorative rim. Cook according to individual recipe instructions.

Peach and Blackberry Cobbler

serves 8

4 cups fresh peaches, pitted, peeled and
   sliced
½ cup sugar
3 tablespoons all-purpose flour
2 tablespoons lemon juice
¼ teaspoon ground nutmeg
2 cups fresh blackberries

Topping
¾ cup firmly packed brown sugar
½ cup softened butter
½ teaspoon salt
1½ cups all-purpose flour
1 cup chopped pecan pieces

Preheat the oven to 375 degrees F.

In a large saucepan, stir the peaches together with the sugar, flour, lemon juice, 2 tablespoons water, and nutmeg. Bring to a boil over medium-high heat, then reduce the heat to medium-low and simmer, stirring occasionally, for 6 to 7 minutes, or until the juices have thickened. Remove the pan from the heat and stir in the blackberries. Spoon the fruit mixture into a lightly-greased 9-inch baking dish.

To make the topping: Stir together the sugar, butter, and salt in a large mixing bowl. Add the flour and pecans and stir until blended. Let the mixture stand about 20 minutes until it crumbles easily into small pieces.

Crumble the topping mixture over the fruit filling and bake for 30 to 35 minutes, or until it is golden brown and the edges are bubbly. Serve with a scoop of vanilla ice cream.

 **RECOLLECTIONS**

One of my childhood memories is of my little brother eating a slice of coconut cream pie at Johnny Harris's—he was six at the time—and liking it so much that he talked our parents into letting him order a second slice. The waiter was a guy named Walter and he cracked up. And he never forgot the incident, either.

Later, my dad would take customers to Johnny Harris's a couple of times a month, and every time, whenever Walter was working, Walter would hand him a slice of pie packed to go "for that little boy of yours." —John Hohenstein

Buttermilk Pie

serves 8

½ cup (1 stick) melted butter
1¾ cups sugar
3 tablespoons all-purpose flour
3 eggs, beaten
1 cup buttermilk

1 teaspoon vanilla extract
¼ teaspoon nutmeg
¼ teaspoon salt
1 unbaked 9-inch deep dish pie crust, or
   The Best Pie Crust, see recipe, p. 185

Preheat the oven to 350 degrees F.

Combine all the ingredients in a large bowl. Whisk until a smooth consistency is reached and then pour into the unbaked pie crust. Bake for 45 to 50 minutes, or until the top is lightly golden and a toothpick inserted in the center comes out clean. Transfer the pie to a wire rack to cool completely, then cover with plastic wrap. The pie may be served warm or refrigerated until it is time to serve.

Caramel Apple Crisp

serves 8

Caramel Topping
¼ cup butter
1 cup brown sugar
½ cup heavy cream
⅛ teaspoon salt
1 tablespoon vanilla extract

½ teaspoon cinnamon
6 large Granny Smith apples, peeled and
   cut into ½-inch slices
⅔ cup all-purpose flour
½ cup packed brown sugar
1 stick cold butter, cut into small pieces
⅔ cup quick cooking oats
1 cup chopped walnuts

To make the caramel topping: combine the butter, brown sugar, cream, salt, and vanilla in a small saucepan over medium-low heat and cook for 7 minutes, or until it thickens. Add the vanilla and cook 1 minute more to thicken. Pour into a lidded container and allow to cool before using.

Preheat the oven to 375 degrees F. In a large bowl, stir together the caramel topping and cinnamon. Stir in the apple slices until all the slices are evenly coated. Spread the apple mixture into an 8-inch square glass baking dish.

Mix the flour and brown sugar into the same bowl that held the caramel apples. Cut in the butter using a knife or a pastry cutter, until the mixture resembles small peas. Stir in the oats and walnuts and sprinkle this over the apples.

Bake for 45 to 50 minutes, until the apples are tender and the topping is golden brown.

Homemade Chocolate Pudding

serves 8

1½ cups chocolate chips
1 cup sugar
4 cups whole milk
6 tablespoons cornstarch

⅛ teaspoon salt
1 tablespoon vanilla extract
2 cups heavy cream
2 teaspoons vanilla sugar

In a heavy saucepan over medium heat, combine the chocolate, sugar, and milk. Heat the mixture slowly, whisking constantly, until the chocolate is melted and smooth. Be careful not to boil. Turn off the heat and pour ½ the heated mixture into a bowl. Stir in the cornstarch and salt until combined. Pour this cornstarch mixture back into the saucepan. Continue stirring over low heat for 8 to 10 minutes, or until the chocolate thickens, then remove from the heat and add the vanilla extract. Allow to cool. (You may refrigerate to hasten the cooling process.)

In the bowl of an electric mixer, whip the heavy cream and the vanilla sugar until stiff. When the pudding has cooled, serve in small bowls and top with whipped cream.

 **RECOLLECTIONS**

Peaches and Cream Bread Pudding

serves 12

12 croissants, cut in 1-inch cubes, or one loaf
   French bread, cut into 1-inch cubes
6 ripe peaches, peeled, pitted and chopped
1 (8-ounce) package cream cheese, cut into
   ½-inch cubes
8 eggs
2 cups milk
1 cup heavy cream
½ cup brown sugar
1 teaspoon vanilla extract
½ teaspoon cinnamon
½ teaspoon salt
¼ teaspoon nutmeg

Caramel Sauce
¾ cup brown sugar
½ cup heavy cream
½ cup butter
2 tablespoons light corn syrup
1 teaspoon vanilla
1 cup chopped pecans, for garnish

Layer a 12 x 9-inch baking dish with the bread, add a layer of peaches and cream cheese on top. If there is enough for a second layer, begin again until all the bread and fruit are used.

Whisk together the eggs, milk, cream, sugar, vanilla, cinnamon, salt, and nutmeg in a large bowl. Pour this mixture evenly over the peaches and bread, cover with plastic wrap, and refrigerate overnight.

Before baking, let the bread pudding stand uncovered at room temperature for 15 minutes.

Preheat the oven to 350 degrees F.

Bake for 40 to 50 minutes, or until set.

To make the caramel sauce: In a medium saucepan over medium-high heat, combine the sugar, cream, butter, and syrup and bring to a boil, whisking occasionally. Reduce the heat to medium and boil gently for 3 minutes. Remove from the heat and add the vanilla. Let cool for 15 minutes, then drizzle the sauce over the pudding and top with the pecans.

Sweet Potato Pie

yields 1 (9-inch) pie

4 cups (6 to 7 medium) sweet potatoes
½ cup butter
½ cup light brown sugar
¼ cup white sugar
½ cup milk
2 eggs

½ teaspoon ground cinnamon
¼ teaspoon ground nutmeg
1 teaspoon vanilla extract
1 (9-inch) Best Pie Crust, unbaked, see recipe,
    p. 185

Preheat the oven to 350 degrees F.

Boil the sweet potatoes whole for 40 to 50 minutes, or until tender. Run cold water over the potatoes and remove the skins. Mash the potatoes with the butter and mix well, using an electric mixer on medium speed. Beat in the sugars, milk, eggs, cinnamon, nutmeg, and vanilla and continue to beat on medium speed until the mixture is smooth.

Pour the filling into the unbaked pie crust and bake for 1 hour, or until a knife comes out clean when inserted in the center. Note: The pie will puff up like a soufflé and then sink down as it cools.

RECOLLECTIONS

My father, Kermit Donaldson, was hired by Johnny Harris in 1927 when he was just a teenager, and eventually he became the owner when Johnny died. It was Johnny who nicknamed him "Red." I was called "Little Red."

When I was still a child, I would work with my father, Red Donaldson, at the restaurant. I remember that every few weeks a man would drive up and my father would tell me, "Go get two bottles of whiskey, put them in a bag, and leave them on the front seat of that man's car when he comes in to talk to me. It's our little gift."

I found out much later that this man was the health inspector for the city.

—Philip Donaldson

Key Lime Pound Cake

serves 12

1 cup (2 sticks) butter, softened
1/2 cup shortening
3 cups sugar
6 large eggs
3 cups all-purpose flour
1/2 teaspoon baking powder
1/8 teaspoon salt
1 cup milk
1 teaspoon vanilla extract
1 teaspoon lime zest
1/4 cup fresh key lime juice

Key Lime Glaze
1 cup powdered sugar
2 tablespoons fresh key lime juice
1/2 teaspoon vanilla extract

Preheat the oven to 325 degrees F.

With an electric mixer on medium speed, beat the butter and shortening until creamy. Gradually add the sugar, beating until the mixture is light and fluffy. Add the eggs, 1 at a time, and beat just until blended after each additional egg.

Stir together the flour, baking powder, and salt in a small bowl. Add the flour mixture to the butter mixture, alternating with the milk, and beginning and ending with the flour. After each addition, beat at low speed until just blended.

Stir in the vanilla, lime zest, and lime juice, and pour the batter into a greased and floured 10-inch (12-cup) tube or Bundt pan. Bake for 75 minutes, or until a long pick inserted into the thickest part of the cake comes out clean. Tranfer the cake pan to a wire rack to cool for 15 minutes, then turn the cake out onto a serving plate.

To make the glaze: Whisk all the ingredients for the glaze until smooth. Using a pastry brush, apply to the top and sides of the warm cake. Continue to cool for 1 hour before serving.

Maudie Belle's Sour Cream Pound Cake

serves 16

My grandmother, Maudie Belle Donaldson, was an excellent cook and spent many hours in the kitchen making delicious meals from scratch for her family. She loved to bake, and this sour cream pound cake was one specialty that was usually found on her holiday table.

3 cups cake flour
1/2 teaspoon baking powder
1/4 teaspoon baking soda
1 cup (2 sticks) butter, softened
2 cups sugar

1 teaspoon vanilla extract
1 teaspoon almond extract
6 eggs
1 cup sour cream

Preheat the oven to 350 degrees F.
  Grease and flour a Bundt pan.
  In a medium bowl, mix together the flour, baking powder, and baking soda and set aside.
  In a separate bowl, beat the butter with an electric mixer at medium speed. Gradually add the sugar, and continue to beat for 6 minutes. The mixture should be light and fluffy and all the the sugar dissolved. Add the vanilla and almond flavorings, then beat in the eggs, 1 at a time. Add the dry ingredients and the sour cream alternately, beating after each addition, just until mixed. Pour the batter into the prepared Bundt pan and bake 1 to 1½ hours, until a toothpick comes out clean when inserted into the center.

Pineapple Coconut Crisp

serves 6

1 fresh pineapple, peeled, cored and
  sliced into bite-size pieces
1 cup all-purpose flour
1/3 cup brown sugar

1/2 cup flaked coconut
1/2 teaspoon salt
1/4 teaspoon nutmeg
6 tablespoons unsalted butter

Preheat the oven to 350 degrees F.
  Butter a 1-quart baking dish. Layer the pineapple pieces in the bottom of the baking dish.

In a small bowl, combine the flour, sugar, coconut, salt, and nutmeg. Cut the butter into this mixture until it is crumbly. Sprinkle evenly over the pineapple and bake for 40 to 45 minutes, or until the top is golden brown. Serve warm with a scoop of vanilla ice cream.

Southern Egg Custard Pie

serves 6 to 8

2 tablespoons butter
1 cup less 2 tablespoons sugar
¼ teaspoon salt
6 eggs
2 cups plus 2 tablespoons whole milk
1½ teaspoons pure vanilla extract, or
   vanilla paste
The Best Pie Crust, unbaked, see recipe, p. 185

Preheat the oven to 450 degrees F.
   Cream the butter, sugar, and salt in a large bowl. Using an electric mixer at medium speed, beat in 3 eggs for 1 minute. Add the other 3 eggs and beat 3 minutes more on high speed. Stir in the milk and blend well. Add the vanilla and stir until blended.
   Pour into a 9-inch, unbaked pie crust and cook for 10 minutes, then reduce the heat to 325 degrees F and continue baking for an additional 25 minutes, or until a knife inserted in the center of the pie comes out clean.

Chocolate Éclair Pie

serves 10 to 12

Pie Crust
½ cup butter
1 cup flour
4 large eggs

Filling
1 (8-ounce) package cream cheese, softened
1 (5.1-ounce) box instant vanilla pudding mix
3 cups milk
1 (8-ounce) container whipped cream
Chocolate syrup, your choice brand
Fresh berries, to garnish

Preheat the oven to 400 degrees F, and lightly grease a 9 x 13-inch glass baking pan.

To make the pie crust: In a medium saucepan over high heat, melt the butter in 1 cup water and bring just to a boil. Remove the pan from the heat and stir in the flour. Mix in the eggs, one at a time, being careful to mix thoroughly before adding the next egg.

Spread the mixture in the pan, covering the sides and bottom evenly. (Make sure the sides are just very slightly greased or the crust will not adhere.) Bake for 30 minutes, or until the crust is golden brown. Check frequently to avoid overcooking. Remove from the oven and allow to cool completely at room temperature. If bubbles have risen in the crust, do not touch or push them down.

To make the filling: Whip the cream cheese in a medium bowl.

In a separate bowl, make the vanilla pudding according to instructions on the box. When the pudding has thickened, slowly stir the pudding into the cream cheese, mixing until there are no lumps. Refrigerate for 1 hour.

Pour the chilled filling into the cooled pie crust. Top with a layer of whipped cream. To serve, cut into squares, drizzle with chocolate syrup, and garnish with fresh berries.

Hot Fudge Pie with Mocha Sauce

serves 8 to 10

4 ounces unsalted butter, plus 1 teaspoon for
  greasing pie plate
1½ squares (1.5 ounces) unsweetened
  baking chocolate
1 cup sugar
2 eggs, beaten
1 teaspoon vanilla extract
2 tablespoons milk
¼ cup all-purpose flour
Ice cream, your choice brand

Mocha Sauce
4 tablespoons butter, melted
1½ tablespoons cocoa
1 tablespoon instant coffee
3 tablespoons milk
½ teaspoon vanilla
1¾ to 2 cups powdered sugar

Preheat the oven to 350 degrees F.

Using 1 teaspoon butter or cooking spray, grease an 8-inch glass or ceramic pie plate.

Melt the butter and chocolate in a saucepan over very low heat until the chocolate is almost entirely melted and then stir. Allow to cool slightly.

In a medium bowl, stir the sugar into the beaten eggs until the sugar is fully incorporated. Mix in the butter-chocolate mixture until completely blended, then add the vanilla and milk. Stir well and beat in the flour, mixing until no white streaks remain. Do not overbeat. Pour into the prepared pie plate and bake for 25 minutes.

To make the mocha sauce: In a small bowl, blend all the sauce ingredients by hand, then using an electric mixer, beat for 30 seconds on medium speed to remove all lumps.

To serve, drizzle 2 tablespoons mocha sauce over a slice of pie and serve with ice cream if desired.

Brown Sugar Pound Cake

serves 8

1 cup shortening
½ cup butter, softened
1 (1-pound) box light brown sugar
5 large eggs
3 cups all-purpose flour
½ teaspoon salt
½ teaspoon baking powder
1 cup evaporated milk
1 teaspoon vanilla extract

Brown Sugar Glaze
½ cup (1 stick) butter
1 cup firmly packed light brown sugar
¼ cup evaporated milk
3 cups powdered sugar
1 teaspoon vanilla extract

Preheat the oven to 300 degrees F.

Beat the shortening, butter, and brown sugar at medium speed with an electric mixer for 2 minutes, or until creamy. Add the eggs, 1 at a time, beating well after each addition. In a separate bowl, combine the flour, salt, and baking powder and add this to the batter, alternating with the milk, and beginning and ending with the flour mixture. Stir in the vanilla extract.

Pour the batter into a greased and floured, 12-cup Bundt pan and bake for 75 minutes, or until a long wooden pick inserted in the center comes out clean. Transfer the pan to a wire rack for 15 minutes to cool, then turn the cake out of the pan and continue to cool on the wire rack.

To make the brown sugar glaze: Melt the butter in a medium saucepan over medium heat. Whisk in the brown sugar and cook for 1 minute. Add the milk, powdered sugar, and vanilla and whisk until creamy. Pour the warm sugar glaze immediately over the cooled cake and let stand for 30 minutes until the glaze has set before serving.

Ambrosia

serves 6

3 large oranges, peeled, seeded, and cut
  into sections
1 large pink grapefruit, peeled, seeded, and
  cut into sections
1 cup pineapple, peeled, cored and cut
  into bite-size pieces
½ cup Maraschino cherries
1 ½ cups flaked coconut, plus more to garnish

½ cup chopped pecans
¾ cup freshly squeezed orange juice
½ cup powdered sugar
½ cup sour cream
1 cup miniature marshmallows

Place the oranges, grapefruit, pineapple, and cherries in a large mixing bowl. Add the coconut and pecans and toss well.

In a small bowl, stir together the orange juice, powdered sugar, and sour cream. Add this to the fruit mixture and toss well to coat. Fold in the marshmallows. Spoon into a large serving dish and sprinkle with a little more coconut to garnish.

Banana Split Cake

serves 12

1 ½ cups graham cracker crumbs
1 ¼ cups sugar
½ cup (1 stick) butter, melted
1 (8-ounce) package cream cheese, softened
1 (20-ounce) can crushed pineapple, drained
6 medium bananas

4 cups cold milk
2 (3.4-ounce) packages vanilla instant pudding
2 cups frozen whipped topping, thawed
1 cup chopped pecans
Chocolate syrup, optional

Mix the cracker crumbs, ¼ cup sugar, and the butter together in a bowl. Press into a 13 x 9-inch pan lined with foil and freeze for 10 minutes.

Meanwhile, use an electric mixer to beat the cream cheese with the remaining 1 cup sugar in a small bowl. Using a spatula, carefully spread the cream cheese mixture over the cooled crust. Top with the crushed pineapple, spreading evenly over the cream cheese. Slice 4 of the bananas into ½-inch-thick slices and arrange in a single layer over the pineapple.

In a large bowl, whisk the milk into the instant pudding mixes, beating for 2 minutes until well blended. Stir 1 cup whipped topping into the pudding and spread the pudding over the banana layer. Spread the rest of the whipped topping over the pudding layer and sprinkle with pecans. Cover and refrigerate for 5 hours.

Just before serving, slice the remaining bananas and arrange 3 to 4 slices atop each serving. Drizzle with chocolate syrup if desired.

Georgia Pecan Cake

serves 12 to 16

1 cup (2 sticks) butter, softened	¾ teaspoon salt
2 cups sugar	½ teaspoon baking powder
4 eggs	½ teaspoon baking soda
1 teaspoon vanilla extract	1 cup buttermilk
½ teaspoon lemon extract	1 cup chopped pecans
3 cups all-purpose flour	Ice cream, optional

In a large mixing bowl, cream the butter and sugar until light and fluffy. Add the eggs, one at a time, beating after each addition. Beat in the extracts.

In a separate bowl, combine the flour, salt, baking powder, and baking soda and set aside ¼ cup. Alternately add the remaining flour mixture and the buttermilk to the butter mixture, stirring to combine.

Toss the pecans with the reserved flour mixture and gently fold into the batter.

Pour into a greased and floured 10-inch tube pan and bake for 60 to 70 minutes. To check for doneness, insert a wooden pick in the center of the cake. If it comes out clean it is ready. Remove from the oven and allow the cake to cool in the pan for 15 to 20 minutes. Run a knife along the inner and outer edges of the tube pan, and invert the cake onto a wire rack.

Serve warm or cold, or with ice cream.

Acknowledgments

It would have been impossible to take on (and finish) a project as all-consuming and involved as writing this book without the understanding, assistance, and encouragement of my wonderful husband, B.J. "Bubba" Lowenthal, Jr. Thank you for your willingness to bring us food from "the big kitchen" on photography days when our own kitchen was closed; and for putting up with my "desk," which seemed to take over the upstairs study, trail down the stairs, and blossom around my computer in the den and onto the sofa and surrounding floor.

A special thanks to my children—Corbin (and Christen!), Brennan, Grayson, and Peyton—who keep me grounded and continue to show me what's truly important in life.

Gratitude to my late grandmother, Maude Donaldson, for giving me free rein in her kitchen, as well as so many priceless memories of good times at "the place."

And to my late grandfather, Kermit "Red" Donaldson, for his hard work and dedication to this restaurant and its customers, which helped create the legacy we carry on today.

A heartfelt thanks to Janice Shay for her careful editing and willingness to walk me through the paper jungle of producing such an all-encompassing book; to Mary Britton Senseney and Marian Cooper Cairns for bringing our recipes to life so beautifully on these pages; and to Polly Powers Stramm for writing a wonderful newspaper article that generated some of the recollections in this book.

Thanks to Robert P. Harrod, whose written history of Johnny Harris helped us fill in the gaps of his story. (His mother, Nellie Syms Harrod, was the checker at Johnny Harris for decades.)

And finally, a huge thank-you to all of our loyal customers, employees, staff, and friends for continuing to make the success of our restaurant possible, and for sharing your stories with us and allowing Johnny Harris to become a part of yours.

Index